Our Response to the Poorest of the Third World

Edited by

ANTHONY JENNINGS
Leicester University, UK

With a Foreword by

The Right Reverend James O'Brien
Bishop in Hertfordshire
President, Commission for International Justice and Peace

PERGAMON PRESS

OXFORD · NEW YORK · TORONTO · SYDNEY · PARIS · FRANKFURT

U.K.	Pergamon Press Ltd., Headington Hill Hall, Oxford OX3 0BW, England
U.S.A.	Pergamon Press Inc., Maxwell House, Fairview Park, Elmsford, New York 10523, U.S.A.
CANADA	Pergamon Press Canada Ltd., Suite 104, 150 Consumers Road, Willowdale, Ontario M2J 1P9, Canada
AUSTRALIA	Pergamon Press (Aust.) Pty. Ltd., P.O. Box 544, Potts Point, N.S.W. 2011, Australia
FRANCE	Pergamon Press SARL, 24 rue des Ecoles, 75240 Paris, Cedex 05, France
FEDERAL REPUBLIC OF GERMANY	Pergamon Press GmbH, Hammerweg 6, D-6242 Kronberg-Taunus, Federal Republic of Germany

First edition 1984

British Library Cataloguing in Publication Data

Jennings, Anthony
Our response to the poorest of the Third World
1. Economic assistance
I. Title
338.91'1722'01724   HC60
ISBN 0-08-030822-8 ✓

Printed in Great Britain by Redwood Burn Ltd., Trowbridge, Wiltshire

Our Response
to the
Poorest of the Third World

Other Titles of Interest

BALASSA, B.
Policy Reform in Developing Countries

COLE, S.
Global Models and the International Economic Order

COREA, G.
Need for Change: Towards the New International Economic Order

FRANKO, L. G. & WEIBER, M. J.
Developing Country Debt

JENNINGS, A. & WEISS, T. G.
The Challenge of Development in the Eighties

MENON, B. P.
Global Dialogue

SAUVANT, K.
Changing Priorities on the International Agenda

STREETEN, P. & JOLLY, R.
Recent Issues in World Development

UNECE
Factors of Growth and Investment Policies

A Related Journal*

WORLD DEVELOPMENT
The multidisciplinary international journal devoted to the study
and promotion of world development

Chairman of the Editorial Board:
Dr. Paul Streeten, Center for Asian Development Studies,
Boston University, USA

*Free specimen copy available on request.

Foreword

The continuation of extreme poverty among the poorest of the Third World is one of the most serious moral dilemmas facing the human family today. We, in the richer countries, have a particular responsibility to respond as generously as possible to the plight of the world's poor.

The Commission for International Justice and Peace of the Roman Catholic Bishops Conference of England and Wales organised a colloquium on Our Response to the Poorest of the Third World at Westminster in November, 1982. The object was to provide a forum where representatives of different interest groups within our society could have an opportunity to reach a deeper under-standing of the problems faced by the poorest of the Third World, and also to discuss the possibilities for more effective action to help them. The papers in the present volume were originally presented at that meeting. We would like to express our gratitude to the individual contributors and to Pergamon Press Ltd. for the publication of the papers in a form which makes them accessible to a wider public. The proceeds from this book will be used by the Commission for International Justice and Peace to foster a continuing dialogue about development in the eighties.

Contents

Contents

Introduction

Background and Summary of the Book

Anthony Jennings

Preoccupation with global negotiations between the rich "North" and the poor "South" tends to conceal the reality of diversity within the two groups. While the solidarity of developing countries in negotiations with the "North" may have assisted in achieving some concessions, there is also a case for recognising their diversity and focusing attention on specific problem areas, for example the poorest of the developing countries. A narrowing of the problem area might then be regarded as more manageable, increasing the possibility of success, rather than sterile confrontation.[1]

The record of North-South co-operation since the call for a new international economic order has not been wholly empty, and assistance to the poorest of the Third World is one area which has seen some progress.[2] Indeed, it could be argued that one area of consensus which has emerged during the Eighties, both at the international and national levels, is that more significant efforts must be made on behalf of the poorest of the Third World. It is one area of the development challenge where zero-sum thinking is obviously wrong, and where morality is so obviously plus national interest, not versus national interest. Alternatively it may be argued that we, the rich, have not as yet appreciated the severity and scale of the problems of the poorest, and the evidence, for example the cutting of funds to the International Development Agency (I.D.A.), a most effective source of multilateral aid for the poorest, denies the existence of a general consensus and conviction to effectively tackle their problems. Development assistance has come under attack from increasingly vocal critics.[3] Even though such attacks may be based "on more or less anecdotal evidence of the occasional failed aid project, or on *a priori* theorising which has little basis in reality,"[4] nevertheless the negative attitude resulting in the North is also to the detriment of the poorest in the South. One observer has likened the North and South to two people in a Harold Pinter play: there they both sit talking right past one another, repeating to themselves and for their own satis- faction the words and phrases they have already used to each other countless times before.[5] It is the basic disagreement over priorities and over the relative importance of different social and moral values, as well as dis- agreement over the distribution of economic values which may be seen as lying behind all the dialogues of the deaf-North-South, East-West, Trans-Atlantic and Trans-Pacific. Are we impotent spectators, or can we, in our different roles in society, contribute to our common future?

1

This volume does not aim at sophisticated academic analysis, but rather
seeks to present in easily understood terms, the response of different
sections of our society as part of the wealthy portion of the globe, to the
needs of the poorest of the Third World. The selection of contributions
does however reflect the belief that an effective strategy requires action
at different levels - global, for example through the United Nations; inter-
regional, for example, through the European Community; and national, through
individuals in their capacities as citizens, trade-unionists, business-
persons, and church-goers. This strategy recognises the interdependence
between the different levels of action necessary for a successful response,
although not surprisingly the representatives of the different interest
groups express different views as to the diagnoses of the problems, and the
prescriptions for their resolution.

The Problems

A Third World perspective on the problems faced by the poorest countries is
given by His Excellency C. M. Mkona, the High Commissioner for Malawi in
London. Since independence in 1964 from its colonial status of Nyasaland,
Malawi has achieved significant advances in development, but even so it
remains one of the poorest countries in the world. Mr. Mkona speaks candidly
when he recognises that some of the poorest countries problems have been of
their own making, for example poor planning, mismanagement and even corruption, but on the whole the problems are not of their making. Problems
frequently arise due to internal factors outside of their control, such as
drought and floods. More serious are the problems suffered due to shocks
originating outside the poorest of the Third World countries, for example
the oil price increases, rising debt service burdens due to higher interest
rates, and inflation imported from developed countries, even before the oil
shocks. Higher import prices and reduced availability of foreign exchange
to import means fewer key imputs for agriculture and hence reduced output.
Protectionist measures preventing their exports to traditional markets
worsen their situation. Squeezed by falling export earnings, and rising
interest payments and import prices, and stagnant aid flows, the poorest are
those least credit worthy for commercial loans. All developing countries
are faced with vicious circles of poverty, but they are the worst for the
poorest.

Daniel W. Caulfield, Chief, Special Programme for Least Developed Countries,
UNCTAD, draws on international comparisons to illustrate the problems faced
by the poorest countries. During the 1970s GDP *per capita* in the least
developed countries - a group of 31 countries covering approximately 13 per
cent of third world population - grew on average by only 0.6 per cent per
annum, and almost half the group were worse off in real terms in 1980 compared with 1970; average adult literacy rate is 26 per cent, while the corresponding rate for all developing countries is 49 per cent; infant mortality
rate is 142 per 1000 live births, compared with 107 per 1000 for all developing countries; life expectancy in the industrialised world is on average
74 years as against 45 years in least developed countries. The problems of
the poorest, while not new, have acquired unprecedented proportions in terms
of the number of human beings affected, and may be seen as part of a systematic malfunction which has accompanied economic and technical progress in
the industrialised world during the past century or so. Mr. Mkona notes that
the figures that are normally quoted to show the gap between the rich and
the poor are at best rather a crude indicator of the differences, but the
figures cannot by themselves convey adequately the harsh realities of hard-
core poverty in the developing world.

In his role as Deputy Director-General for Development, European Community,

Mr. Maurice Foley highlights the plight of the poorest countries whose economy depends on a single commodity - such as coffee or cocoa - and when its price falls on the world market they encounter indifference and selfishness in the developed world. Other poorest countries have little to sell to the outside world, and theirs is a problem of survival. Mr. Foley criticises the duplicity of rich countries which offer aid to the poorest on the one hand yet also deny them access to their markets. He also criticises complicated aid procedures which benefit the development theorists and consultants of the rich, and simply fill the shelves of Ministers of Finance, and Prime Ministers with studies paid for out of development aid money but never read or put into practice.

Timothy Eggar, MP, Parliamentary Private Secretary to the Minister of Overseas Development states that the biggest driving force towards development remains the determination and political will within the recipient country itself that the lot of its people will be bettered. However the British government's official aid programme is substantial, exceeded by only five other donors, and as a percentage of GNP above average compared with other OECD donors. A problem constraining the growth of our aid commitment for poverty-focused projects is the recipients' inadequate management capacity. Dependence upon expatriate skills to launch and run such schemes can be counter-productive, and building up national institutions can be a necessary preliminary stage. Regrettably, the weight of public opinion against aid, as well as our underlying economic situation, also inevitably puts restraints on development and aid policy. Giving an Opposition view, Kevin McNamara, MP and former Chairman of the Select Committee on Overseas Development, argues that private investment can have little return in the poorest countries, and so increased aid volume and quality were essential. Unfortunately the Conservative Government had abandoned aid volume targets, switched aid policy to trade, political and defense criteria away from the poorest, and downgraded the role of overseas development.

Sir Reay Geddes, a Deputy Chairman of the Midland Bank, gives his perception of the problems of the poorest countries which limit severely the growth of an enterprising domestic commercial sector. Resources are needed to alleviate poverty and too little is left for human and physical infrastructure to build up directly productive investment to eradicate it. Foreign business has little scope to bring in productive resources so the main burden of priming the pump for development rests with government and voluntary organisations. What, if anything, can be done by foreign business to come in at an earlier stage of development than happens now?

Mr. David Lea, Assistant General Secretary, TUC, recognises that there is a groundswell of Trade Union support for protecting particular industries against cheaper imports and this poses problems for poor countries. However the underlying cause of the protectionist trend is high world unemployment which is a tragic waste of human and capital resources and a reflection of an inadequate arrangement of our affairs in the world. He also argues that in all parts of the world where there is an active trade union movement based on democratic principles, there is a more equal distribution of income and wealth.

Geoffrey Wilson, the Chairman of Oxfam details the problems faced by the voluntary agencies in the rich world, and in the poorest countries. In the UK, the law and its watchdogs, the Charity Commissioners, constrain their efforts to educate and make our fellow citizens aware of the needs of the poorest. Sometimes we feel that their voices are small and unheard "in the awful wilderness of our own unemployment and other home problems." Some-

times their overseas projects may seem to be in danger of being swamped by
mammoth programmes, rapacious landlords, drought and many other dangers.
He wryly observes how well meaning, but often clumsy, unimaginative and
insensitive our own modern welfare state is at helping the poorest in our
own society, so not surprisingly helping the poorest overseas, programmes
often are inappropriate and unsuccessful.

Accepting that we have the technical know-how and resources available to
eliminate the worst excesses of poverty, the continuation of extreme poverty
reflects, in the words of the Archbishop of Canterbury, the Right Reverend
R. Runcie, the fact "that we - as a society, represented by our Government -
have yet to take on board the enormity of the developing world's problems ...
the 800 million people, for example who, in the words of Robert MacNamara,
former President of the World Bank, are living 'in situations so deprived as
to be below any rational definition of human decency'; or the 17 million
children who die each year, many of whom could be saved by the expenditure
of relatively small sums on basic health care." The Archbishop states that
we are in danger of becoming moral abstainers on what is fundamentally a
moral issue. This view is echoed by many contributors including Maurice
Foley who suggests that "without that moral influence we will simply play
around between Conservatives and Labour arguing together, but not taking
strong effective action because there are no votes in it." The Archbishop
of Canterbury senses "a real crisis of confidence among those who work in
the development field ... not only do they feel hamstrung by the lack of
resources, but they feel that they must battle constantly against official
lack of support."

Solutions

The need for solutions based on a recognition of the interdependence of
developed and developing countries, and particularly the poorest developing
countries, is a recurring theme throughout the contributions. Mr. Mkona
astutely re-echoes the plea made by the Governor of the Bank of England for
a long term perspective in a world of increasing interdependence in respect
of trade, of capital flows, and of the international exposure of banks.
Mr. Mkona emphasises three areas where more effective international co-operative action could improve the prospect for success of domestic policies *viz*
more stable exchange rates of reserve currency countries, reverse the trend
to protectionism, and increase the resources available to, and effectiveness
of, international financial institutions in assisting countries to adopt
appropriate adjustment policies. Such actions are not a matter of just
charity.

Mr. Caulfield reminds us that the Substantial New Programme of Action adopted
by the international community at the Paris UN Conference on Least Developed
Countries in 1981 already provides a framework for tackling the problems of
many of the poorest countries at the national and international level. The
"rich" committed themselves to either doubling, or raising to 0.15 per cent
of GNP, their aid to the least developed countries by 1985, as well as
improving the quality of their aid by, for example, providing more programme
aid. Latest statistics unfortunately indicate that aid to this poorest
group of countries has in fact declined. Mr. Caulfield warns that early
delivery on commitments is essential not only to prevent a worsening of
poverty, but also to avoid the fatal erosion of the credibility of our
international institutions.

The UK as a member of the European Community contributes to their existing
development policy through the Lome Agreements which channels about two
thousand million dollars to developing countries, and is due for renegotia-

tion. Mr. Foley suggests that the only appropriate response to the poorest
of the poor is to reach them quickly, and he suggests creating a "petty-
cash account" to put at their disposal. Such projects as feeder roads,
storage facilities, fertiliser imports, and training at a local level should
be supported, and not prestige projects such as hydroelectric dams and major
motorways."

The focus of the British government's contribution to the poorest is
primarily via the aid programme, and Mr. Eggar notes an increase in its
real value for 1983 as compared with 1982, and defends its high quality as
being respected world-wide. He makes no pretence that political, commercial
and industrial factors are not important in determining aid policy, but
they are "alongside" developmental objectives. Less than half of UK aid is
tied to purchase of UK goods and services, a figure determined by political
realities, in particular the taxpayer, and measures are being taken to
reduce the spiralling export credit race. About two-thirds of UK bilateral
and multilateral aid does go to the poorest countries, and finances projects
and programmes which benefit the poorest people in these countries.

Mr. McNamara emphasises the need for the industrialised countries of the
North, including Comecon, to take concertive efforts to solve the problems
of the poorest. He highlights the absolute commitment of the next Labour
Government to increase the amount of money in overseas aid, and to help alter
the quality of life of the poorest of the poor. Also they will seek to
identify and eliminate those obstacles in procedures and forums which delay
and frustrate the North-South dialogue.

In assessing possible solutions Sir Reay Geddes raises the interesting
possibility that progress might be faster if priority were given to advance
by salients, rather than spreading scarce resources over even a moderately
wide front. Also the principle of "graduation" should be built into the
development processes, part of what he prefers to call the Evolving International Economic Order. Subject to the reality of the constraints on
business operation - for example the need to make profits to survive - the
contribution of foreign business may be direct through community projects,
as well as their chosen business, and indirect, for example the considerable
lending by financial institutions. The problem-solving and administrative
ability of foreigners, including business executives could also be harnessed
to help the poorest.

The response of Trade Unions to the desperate problems of the poorest are
categorised by Mr. Lea as firstly using their influence nationally and
internationally to persuade decision-makers to adopt policies appropriate to
economic and social development, especially expansionary policies and
increased aid, and secondly using their experience to work directly with
colleagues in Trades Unions in the Third World to help them build up their
own organisations. Their grass-roots credibility makes Trade Unions important partners in mobilising national resources behind economic goals, in
upholding democratic freedoms and basic human rights, and in acting as a
bridge in the North-South dialogue.

The non-governmental organisations have long been in the vanguard of helping
the poor. Sir Geoffrey Wilson explains how their characteristics of being
non-political, flexible, sensitive, willing to experiment, to share experiences, and to act as a catalyst, combine to make them one of the most
effective agents for assisting development of the poorest in the Third
World. Taking an Oxfam project as an example he emphasises their use of
local but improved techniques, and other local resources.

The Right Reverend Runcie argues for a greater involvement of Christians in helping the poorest on the basis of the non-negotiable principle that parallel to the pursuit of brotherhood is the pursuit of justice for all those embraced by the fatherhood of God and the brotherhood of man. There are many ways to demonstrate a Christian concern from service in the poorest countries, to raising money in a jumble sale. While recognising the significant contributions we already make in aid and trade, the Archbishop calls on the Government not to become obsessed with development at the expense of humanitarian aid. To dispel the suspicions of offical indifference, and to reverse the trend to moral abstention, the Archbishop calls on Government to clearly express its commitment and energy to assist poorer nations, for example by raising the Minister of Overseas Development to Cabinet-status, giving more aid, and to initiate the launching of a new Marshall Plan.

Each contributor emphasises the need for arousing greater public awareness about the issues, so that, for example, development of the poorest countries becomes an election issue, and the person who believes in the third world ceases to be regarded as a dreamy idealist. Mr. Foley observes that "politicians will move when public indignation makes them move and that public indignation is a question of conscience." Others see the issue, not between those who are for and those who are against development (not only aid), but those who can join hands because, for their different combinations of reasons, they are all for prosperity. The International Broadcasting Trust, Centre for World Development Education and trade union education and training are all mentioned as worthy of further support. Sir Reay Geddes suggests that it may be timely to re-think the underlying general appeal for world development, and questions whether as yet we have "a clear and persuasive call likely to move worried governments, harassed managers, anxious trade unionists and preoccupied voters to do or support the right things?"

In the final chapter, Professor Hans Singer, Emeritus Professor, University of Sussex, and Professorial Fellow, Institute of Development Studies, contributes his reflections on the different responses to the poorest of the Third World, based on many years of working in the cause of development at national and international level. He raises the paradox that at a time of high unemployment it may be argued that we must first put our own house in order before we presume to help others. However it is also the best time to increase aid to the poorest since otherwise the resources would be wasted. The normal self-interest activity especially in trade, commerce and finance does not really reach the poorest countries and therefore we must go beyond immediate self-interest. Professor Singer makes a special plea to help "children" in poverty, as part of our common heritage.

It is for the reader to judge, having weighed the various contributions to this book from the different interest groups represented, whether society will make a just response to the poorest of the Third World. The book may be criticised as failing to present a coherent strategy. If this is so, perhaps it is because we, as a society, do not have one. A variety of responses to this most urgent challenge are not only possible but also may be necessary. The conclusion of an assessment of Our Response to the Challenge of Development in The Eighties applies even more so in the case of our response to the Poorest of the Third World, namely that self-satisfaction and inaction are the only unacceptable responses.

References

1. T. G. Weiss and A. Jennings, *More for the Least? Prospects for the Poorest Countries in the Eighties*, Lexington, Mass., D. C. Heath, 1983 pp. 177.

2. The Independent Commission on International Development Issues, *Common Crisis: North-South, Co-operation for World Recovery*, Pan, 1983.

3. P. Bauer and B. Yamey, *The Political Economy of Foreign Aid*, Lloyds Bank Review, October, 1981.

4. R. Cassen, *Address to the British Association for the Advancement of Science*, Section F, August, 1983.

5. Susan Strange, The Poverty of Multi-lateral Economic Diplomacy, in G. Berridge and A. Jennings (Eds.), *The United Nations and Diplomacy*, Macmillan Press Ltd., 1984.

Chapter 1

A Third World Perspective

His Excellency C. M. Mkona, High Commissioner for Malawi in
London

The Problems facing the Poorest in the Third World

The needs of the World's poorest countries in the eighties have been a
constant and continuous topic for innumerable and varied conferences. There
are today volumes and volumes of reports on this very subject.[1] The following presents the problems faced by the poorest of the Third World countries
in order to see the problems in a more balanced perspective, so that it may
be easier to understand our expectations from the developed world.

The obstacles to development faced by the Third-World are indeed real, and
particularly the difficult economic, budgetary and balance of payments
problems with which most, if not all, Third-World countries, and even some
developed countries, are faced. Firstly, it is probably true that some of
the problems could have been avoided, but the problems are not always of our
own making. In most cases they have originated from outside the poorest of
the Third-World countries and must, therefore, be seen in the context of
world wide financial problems. Secondly, even when the problems come from
within, i.e. domestic, very often they are beyond the control of those
responsible. Unfavourable weather conditions are a good example.

"Problems" which have come about because of external factors, and, therefore,
are not of the poorest of the Third-World countries' making include:

(a) *Oil Shock*

All Third-World countries, indeed like all developed countries, must
use oil. The "oil shock", particularly that of 1978/79, and the
subsequent world wide "stag-flation" triggered a series of economic
problems with which most Third-World countries are faced today. In
most cases the oil import bills have more than doubled between 1978
and 1981 even when some countries, like my own, are exercising strict
discipline over fuel consumption. For countries whose economies are
closely linked with agriculture, this terrible rise in oil prices has
meant that imports of essential agricultural inputs, such as fertili-
sers and pesticides, have also become more expensive. Because of the
"oil shock", import prices rose higher and consequently a sharp
deterioration in their terms of trade was experienced by many Third-
World countries.

This situation is not particular to Third-World countries, but Third-
World countries are the worst hit by it. Because of the higher import
prices in countries dependent on agriculture, for instance, other
sectors of the economy were in turn affected. The decrease in key
inputs for agriculture and the resulting poor harvests has meant less
income for the majority of the people and the reduction of raw
materials for the agro-based manufacturing and processing firms.

Moreover, reduced harvest means less availability for exports and
reduction of Government's ability to raise revenues. The situation can
be even worse if the weather conditions are poor. Poor weather in most
Third-World countries, (and even in the developed ones), aggravates the
situation as it further weakens the country's ability to export and
necessitates the import of staple foods with consequent budgetary and
balance of payments implications, and complications.

(b) Increase in Interest Rates
Another factor complicated the already difficult economic, budgetary
and balance of payments problems, namely the sharp increase in interest
rates on commercial loans. For instance, the London Interbank Borrowing Rate increased by nearly half between 1979 and 1981. The heavier
debt service burden added to the balance of payments problem at a time
of continued decline in terms of resource availability for many
countries in the Third-World. It was this factor in the final analysis
which brought about the balance of payments and the budgetary situations
with which many Third-World countries are faced. For Malawi, the repay-
ment of principal plus interest as a proportion of exports of goods and
non factor services rose rapidly from 11.3 per cent in 1978 to 44 per
cent in 1982. This is excluding public short term debts and private
sector debt. If these are included, the proportion of pre-committed
export earnings in the form of debt servicing would be much higher still.
The problem of debt servicing has also serious implications for the
budget. In Malawi, in the 1978/79 fiscal year, for example, debt
servicing was 15 per cent of total expenditure on the recurrent account.
This ratio has since risen to 40 per cent in 1981/82. If the increase
in prices over the years is allowed for, it is easy to see the extent to
which a country's budget has been severely strained by debt servicing.

(c) Inflation
Although I have argued that the "Oil Shock" triggered a series of
economic problems with which most Third-World countries are faced
today, perhaps I should have given prominence to inflation which had
set in even before the first "Oil Shock", and which the Third-World
countries had imported from the developed countries. Indeed the high
rates of inflation in the industrial world contributed importantly to
the increase in total costs of imports purchased even before the "Oil
Shock."

For most Third-World countries, particularly the non-oil developing
countries, the global economic environment of the past several years
has been very difficult. The international recession has limited the
growth of export markets and adversely affected terms of trade. Many
of them continued to try and expand their fiscal and monetary policies
during these hard times, thus generating excessive domestic demands
that inevitably spilled into imported products. In order to finance
the resulting larger flow of imports, as well as the imports essential
for maintenance of minimal domestic growth, and to do so at a time of
unusually weak expansion of export earnings, most of these countries

have had to increase their external borrowing substantially since
1978. These countries were only able to deal with a portion of this
huge increment in financing requirements by ceasing to accumulate
reserves and by obtaining enlarged inflows of funds in various forms
that do not create debt. But even so they had to borrow extensively
mainly from private financial institutions in order to finance their
current account deficits.

The World Bank in its World Development Report, 1982, observes that
inflation has over the past decade, accelerated, and interest and
exchange rates have become more volatile, because inflation affects the
value and significance of certain balance of payments items in several
ways. First, it reduces the real impact of nominal increases in
current account deficits and debt. Secondly, when interest rates on a
country's debt are not fully adjusted for inflation, a country's overall current account position may not be an accurate reflection of the
change in the real value of its net external assets. It is reported
that the inflation rate is dropping in most of the developed countries.
In the non-oil developing countries, however, inflation may come down,
but the projected change is not very large. It would still not change
things very much.

The foregoing examples relate to development problems which have come about
because of factors emanating from outside the poorest of Third-World
countries. It is clear from these examples that something ought to be done.
The balance of payments has to be strengthened and the fiscal and monetary
equilibrium restored. I could have considered the Bretton Woods arrangements which had played a very important role in regulating international
financial relations in the post-war years, but which, everyone agrees, has
become unsustainable. But I leave that to the international financial
experts. I could also have considered some of the internal factors, such
as poor planning, mismanagement and even corruption, but I do not think it
is necessary, because this would entail considerable detail, which I lack.

The Solution
It is clear that a solution to the problems faced by Third-World countries
must be found. In order to highlight the urgency of finding a solution, I
can do no better than quote from the speech of the Governor of the Bank of
England, The Rt. Hon. Gordon Richardson, MBE, TD., at the Lord Mayor's
Dinner in honour of the Bankers and Merchants of the City of London:

"I need scarcely say that it is not we in the developed world alone
who are affected. World recession on the present scale has fallen
with especial force on the developing countries. The prices of
commodities are now lower in real terms than at any time in the last
30 years. This may seem convenient for us in that we pay less for
imported materials, and inflation is reduced. But for those who
produce them, it means lower incomes, forcing them to cut imports.
The position of different developing countries differs markedly.
Most - and certainly the poorest - have little access to international capital markets. Their current balance of payments deficits
have been limited by the availability of official finance; and they
have had no option but to try to adjust to the worsening situation.
For others the impact of falling commodity prices has been compounded
by the burden of the external debt - most of it banking debt - they
have incurred over the last decade. International financial
institutions are there to see that countries are not unnecessarily
driven by financial difficulties to actions which would damage world

> trade or the structure of international credit. These institutions
> have a unique role in assisting countries to adopt appropriate
> adjustment policies. Their share in financing will need to increase
> relative to that provided by commercial banks, and they must there-
> fore have sufficiently large resources to meet that enlarged share,
> ... I have sought to show that our problems, severe as they are, must
> be seen in a long perspective and in the context of a world of
> increasing interdependence in respect of trade, of capital flows and
> of the international exposure of banks."

I can do no better than re-echo the plea made by the Governor of the Bank of
England. Countries in the world, developed and developing, are interrelated
and interdependent. Success in one country or in a set of countries is
likely to have favourable repercussions elsewhere, and vice versa. By
Interdependence, it does not mean one country being charitable to another.
A more appropriate view is to regard the world as being a big clock. If all
the parts are in good working order, then the clock is in good order; all
the parts together make the clock. It is not a matter of just charity
that the other parts should do their role. Although some countries may
refuse to recognise publicly the fact that the countries of the world are
interdependent because they feel that they are better off, or are more
superior, or are oil-producing, or are maritime nations or are the older
ones, etc., it is a fact that all the countries of the world are interdependent. Aid given in one way or another may end being in the interest
of the donor as well as the receiver.

The economies of most of the Third-World countries are faced with a number
of problems which cannot be resolved in a short period of time. Any
stabilisation programmes adopted must have a medium-term frame, the
principal objectives being to promote the re-emergence of growth, improve
the financial position and to restore the balance of payments to a sustain-
able level over the medium term. Such programmes should probably envisage
a wide range of policies aimed at curbing demand, stimulating production
and promoting exports. It is therefore in these fields, and others related
to these, that Third-World countries would need the developed countries'
cooperation directed at restoring and reviving their severely battered
economies, and also closing the gap between the rich and the poor countries.

Faced with such severe problems, Third-World countries have had to improvise
and do something to avoid bankruptcy, but most of the problems cannot be
resolved in a short period of time. Any adjustment programmes will tend
to have a medium-term time frame. Some of the Third-World countries have
had to devalue in order to provide increased price incentives for export
products, besides rationalising import demand, and encouraging a search for
domestic substitutes for imported raw materials. These developing
countries have also taken measures to reduce the fiscal deficit despite
increased costs caused by the devaluation, such as by lower allocations for
purchases of goods and services, a cut in the Government contingency funds,
a reduction in domestically financed Government construction outlays, and
imposing of taxes. Some have launched their stabilisation programmes
supported by stand-by arrangements with the IMF and programmes of economic
recovery supported by structural adjustment loans from the World Bank.
Quite a number of the Third-World countries, in view of their heavy debt
obligations, have requested for a rescheduling of publicly guaranteed
foreign debts in the hope that such a rescheduling would provide relief to
the balance of payments.

We urgently need agreement on concrete recommendations towards the framing

of national and international policies in the critical question of providing
greater opportunity for development to the developing countries and of the
progressive removal of the widening disparities of wealth between the rich
and poor countries. I would like to re-emphasise three important areas
where more effective international cooperative action could improve the
prospect for success of domestic policies in different countries:[2]

(a) *Exchange Rates*
     The uncertainty created by the volatility of exchange rates has been
     inimical to growth. It is generally recognised that it is the
     responsibility of reserve currency countries, in the interests of
     stability, to maintain the internal and external value of their
     currencies.

(b) *Trade*
     There is pressing need for more cooperative international action in the
     field of trade. Despite the role played by GATT there are increasing
     manifestations of protectionism appearing everywhere. It is hoped that
     GATT will address itself seriously to this problem.

(c) *International Financial Institutions*
     These institutions are there to see that countries are not unnecess-
     arily driven by financial difficulties to actions which would damage
     world trade or the structure of international credit. These institu-
     tions have a unique role in assisting countries to adopt appropriate
     adjustment policies. Their share in financing will need to increase
     relative to that provided by commercial banks, and they must therefore
     have sufficiently large resources to meet that enlarged share.

Finally, I would like to quote a paragraph from a Commonwealth Secretariat
Report entitled *Towards a New International Order:*

     "The effective implementation of a new order calls for firm commit-
     ments from all parties to match rhetoric with concrete action.
     Starting from the perspective of self-reliance, the developing
     countries can, by individual and collective action, demonstrate their
     new resolve to achieve the fullest possible mobilisation of their
     resources for development. The developed countries, especially those
     with balance of payments surpluses, are well placed to take a lead in
     supporting the efforts of developing countries aimed at generating
     greater strength in the world economy. The centrally planned
     economies can play an important role through appropriate improvements
     in the geographical coverage and in the content of trade, economic
     and financial agreements with developing countries."

It may not be possible to bridge the gap between the rich and the poor
nations overnight. The figures which are normally quoted to show the gap
between the rich and the poor in terms of *per capita* GNP are at best a
rather crude indicator of the differences, but the figures cannot by themselves convey adequately the harsh realities of hard-core poverty in the
developing world. It is up to the developed countries to see that at least
the basic requirements of every human being are achieved, including,
sufficient food, adequate clothing and housing, good health and education.

References
1. Recent reports include:
    - Towards a New International Economic Order, by the Commonwealth
       Secretariat.

- The Brandt Commission Report: North/South, A Programme for Survival, (1980) and Common Crisis: North-South: Co-operation For World Recovery, (1983).

- The Report on the U.N. Conference on Least Developed Countries held in Paris, September, 1981.

- World Economic Outlook, (Occasional Paper 9), by IMF staff.

- World Development Report 1983 by the World Bank.

2. These recommendations are also in the speech which was delivered by the Governor of the Bank of England, The Rt. Hon. Gordon Richardson, at the Lord Mayor's Dinner in honour of the Bankers and Merchants of the City of London on 21st October, 1982. In this speech he was not speaking particularly on behalf of the Third-World countries, on the contrary he was addressing the Bankers and Merchants of the City of London.

Chapter 2

The International Community and the Poorest of the Third World

Daniel W. Caulfield, Chief, Special Programme for Least
Developed, Land-locked and Island Developing Countries,
UNCTAD, Geneva

The problems of the poorest are certainly not new. They form part of a
systematic malfunction which has accompanied economic and technological
progress in the industrialised parts of the world during the past century
or so. Phenomena such as mass poverty, starvation, high mortality rates,
and so forth, have been general throughout the history of mankind. The
novelty of the present situation, however, is that while such problems per-
sist in large areas of the world, they have been eradicated elsewhere and,
it can be said, could be eradicated everywhere. Modern technology and
productivity levels make it possible to envisage their eradication. In
spite of this, they have acquired unprecedented proportions in terms of the
number of human beings affected. Disparities in the living conditions of
the richer and those of the poorest continue to widen. The perception that
we all have of such problems is clearer than ever before and, therefore, our
responsibility to react is inevitably stronger. Moreover, what is newest,
the problems of the poorest have been aggravated, and continue to be aggravated, by the economic crisis which is taking place in the richer areas of
the world. The poorest are thus being badly hit and penalised for something
for which they cannot be held responsible. Their efforts to develop are
thereby nullified, and their hopes at best dramatically postponed.

Times are difficult indeed, and from all sides we perceive manifestations
of economic and social malaise. Unemployment rates in the developed world
are attaining peak levels, and protectionism is growing again. Inflation
rates are not being checked without creating simultaneously the spectre of
a new crisis like that of the 1930s. The debt position of a growing number
of countries has attained levels which put at stake the very continuance of
the prevailing international financial structure. Against this background,
can the international community afford to pay attention to the problems of
the poorest, whilst all countries are striving to cope with their own
problems?

The answer can only be yes. Not only for the sake of solidarity with the
deprived, a principle which has formed part of the outstanding values of
our civilisation. Not only because of commitments made by the international
community after long, and often difficult, negotiations. But also on the
grounds of everybody's interest in the long run.

International inequity and mass poverty are indeed major sources (though
not the only ones, it is true) of tension in today's world. Tensions which
often flourish, and understandably, in the poorest areas of the world. The
importance of these areas for world stability and peace cannot, in fact, be
measured shortsightedly in terms of market size, of absorption capacity, of
financial potential. These areas form part of our world and, therefore,
they can be a source of equilibrium, or of disequilibrium. They participate in major international negotiations and decisions. They are striving
seriously and energetically to overcome their economic and social problems.
They are looking for viable peaceful solutions, with admirable hope and
faith. Their disappointment would entail the disappointment of a large
portion of mankind, and, perhaps, a fatal erosion of the credibility of
present institutions and mechanisms as they have prevailed in the post-war
period.

I will concentrate on the problems affecting the poorest countries amongst
the poor of the world. They do not, of course, cover the totality of the
poorest of this earth. We all know that the problems of mass poverty,
starvation, sub-human living conditions also occur in other parts of the
world. The question of meeting basic needs everywhere is indeed another
major source of preoccupation for the international community. This question forms part of the subjects of concern of many institutions and agencies
and is one of the essential targets of the New International Economic Order.
As regards the poorest countries, the international community has not been
indifferent to their problems. Both multilateral and bilateral mechanisms
of assistances have been created to assist them since the end of World War
II. Areas covered are as varied as food, health, education, trade, finance,
technology, and technical co-operation. In many cases, arrangements relate
to the Third World as a whole or to a group thereof, and they are therefore
applicable to all or some of the poorest among the developing countries.
Such arrangements include tariff preferences, the target of allocating
0.7 per cent of gross national product of developed countries to be provided
to the Third World as official development assistance (ODA) and the Lomé
Convention, which provides for assistance and co-operation between the
European Community and developing countries of Africa, Asia and the
Caribbean. In the negotiation of these and other arrangements, the Third
World has monolithically stood behind its poorest members so that their
special problems be recognised, and their needs met, in an appropriate
manner.

As a way of concentrating attention on the poorest, a list of countries has
been drawn by the United Nations, and it comprises those countries which
combine the lowest levels of *per capita* income with the lowest share of
manufacturing in GDP and the lowest literacy rates. These countries are
named the least developed countries of the world. The "unfortunate club"
has increased in membership from 25 in the early 1970s to 31 at present.
Seven of these countries form part of the Asia and Pacific region, one is
in Latin America, and the remainder are located in the African continent.
Their total population covers approximately 13 per cent of the population of
the Third World, and 6 per cent of that of the world as a whole. The
General Assembly of the United Nations is considering, and will most likely
approve, the inclusion of five more countries to the list.*

---

*At the thirty-seventh session of the General Assembly five countries -
 Djibouti, Equatorial Guinea, Sao Tomé and Principe, Sierra Leone and
 Togo - were added to the list.

Of crucial significance in this context is the holding by the United Nations, in Paris in September 1981, of a Conference on the Least Developed Countries. The Conference adopted unanimously the "Substantial New Programme of Action" for the Least Developed Countries in the 1980s, or SNPA, with the objectives of transforming their economies toward self-sustained development and enabling them to provide at least internationally accepted minimum standards of nutrition, health, transport and communications, housing and education as well as job opportunities to all their citizens. The adoption of the SNPA constitutes without doubt a major breakthrough in the search for an effective response by the international community to the acute problems of the least developed countries.

The SNPA consolidates and strengthens relevant commitments which had been made earlier by the international community on different occasions. In it, the least developed countries adhere to guidelines for action by themselves at the national level. It further provides for measures of international support to complement action at the national level through increased financial resource transfers and through policies and programmes affecting the modalities of assistance, technical assistance, transfer of technology, commercial policy measures and co-operation among developing countries.

An overall review of the implementation of the SNPA is to be undertaken in the mid 1980s. Meanwhile, however, it is appropriate to watch carefully whatever steps are being taken in this respect so as to identify whether or not they are sufficient to achieve the objectives of the SNPA, whether commitments are being actually met, and whether the courses of action are the appropriate ones.

In this connection, in October, 1982, a report was presented to the General Assembly by the Secretary-General of the United Nations on the implementation of the SNPA. On the basis of the information now available, UNCTAD is very concerned about the continuing deterioration in the economic situation of the least developed countries as well as about the slow pace at which the SNPA is being implemented.

During the 1970s GDP *per capita* in these countries grew on average by 0.8 per cent per year. In 1980, their average GDP *per capita* reached an estimated level of 222 dollars, as compared with 982 dollars for all developing countries, 4,503 dollars for socialist countries of Eastern Europe, and 9,675 dollars for developed market economy countries. For almost half of the least developed countries, however, GDP *per capita* was actually lower in real terms in 1980 than in 1970. And in 1981, average GDP *per capita* for the least developed group as a whole decreased by 0.6 per cent.

All recent data point to the severe situation of these countries. A few examples may be relevant. The average consumption *per capita* of energy amounts to 48 kg. of coal equivalent, as compared to 437 kg. of coal equivalent for developing countries as a whole. The average adult literacy rate is 26 per cent, while the corresponding rate for all developing countries is 49 per cent. And the average infant mortality rate is 142 per 1000 live births for the least developed countries and 107 per 1000 for all developing countries as a whole. And while a human being of the industrial world can expect to live 74 years, the average life expectancy at birth of his brother or sister from a least developed country is only 45 years.

At Paris, it was clearly recognised that the least developed countries would not be able to mobilise sufficient resources domestically for the purpose

of implementing the Substantial New Programme of Action. It was also
agreed that only a substantial increase in official development assistance
in real terms during the present decade would enable the least developed
countries to achieve the objectives of their country programmes. Further-
more, the SNPA stated that as large a proportion as possible of these
increased transfers of resources should be disbursed urgently and effectively in order to meet immediate needs and to provide the necessary
momentum to the development efforts of the least developed countries.

In order to achieve this result, donors agreed at the Paris Conference to
make a special effort to increase their contributions. All donor countries
reaffirmed their commitment to the target of 0.7 per cent of gross national
product to be provided as overall official development assistance. And
such flows are to be directed increasingly towards the least developed
countries. Specifically in this connection most donors of official development assistance would devote in the coming years 0.15 per cent of their
gross national product to the least developed countries. Others agreed to
double their official development assistance to the least developed
countries in the same period. It was stated in the SNPA that taken together,
these efforts would be likely to achieve, by 1985, a doubling of official
development assistance to the least developed countries, compared to the
transfers to them during the last 5 years.

In 1981 bilateral ODA from DAC member countries to least developed countries
decreased in current terms from 3.24 billion dollars to 3.16 billion
dollars, remaining thus on the average at 0.04 per cent of donors' GNP.
In that same year DAC contributions to multilateral agencies decreased by
almost 20 per cent, while the share of flows allocated to least developed
countries by these agencies did not increase. Overall DAC ODA, which
accounted on the average for 0.07 per cent of donors' GNP in 1980, thus
moved backward from the 0.15 target during that year. According to the
latest data available, OPEC concessional flows to the least developed
countries in 1981, both bilateral and through multilateral agencies,
similarly fell in current terms from 790 million to 605 million dollars.
Taking into account the adverse effects of inflation would make the picture
look even worse.

In the light of the above considerations, it is absolutely necessary to find
ways and means of accelerating the flows of resources towards the least
developed countries. Early delivery of commitments made in Paris by donor
countries and institutions becomes very important in this respect.

Another important area which requires immediate action concerns improvement
in aid practices and management. This issue relates in particular to terms
and conditions of aid; to adapting assistance criteria to the specific needs
of the LDCs; to non-project aid, local cost financing and recurrent
financing; to administration and management of aid programmes; and to
technical assistance. These matters were dealt with at a meeting of multilateral and bilateral financial and technical assistance institutions with
representatives of the least developed countries, which was held in Geneva
from 11 to 20 October, 1982. Detailed recommendations and guidelines are
contained in the report of that meeting.

From all these considerations it follows that the impoverishment of the least
developed countries will not be overcome and redressed unless the international community strengthens its co-operation in a manner and a measure
consonant with the commitments made at Paris. A series of international

meetings are scheduled to be held during the 1980s to review progress made
in the implementation of the SNPA, on a country-by-country basis and also
at the global level.

They provide a major opportunity to test the willingness of the international community to strengthen support to these countries' endeavours.

From past experience, it is clear that the governments of the richer
countries will not manifest the necessary political will unless their
public opinion induces them to do so. Not infrequently, those governments
express reluctance on the grounds that their constituencies could hardly
accept further disbursements for the poorest at times when their own
countries are undergoing major economic problems. It is, therefore, those
who perceive more clearly the intricacies and interdependences at stake who
need to do their utmost within their own countries to indicate the reasons
and advantages of demonstrating a more active solidarity with the
unprivileged of the world. The non-governmental sector of developed
countries has thus a crucial role to play in securing a responsive attitude
on the part of their respective governments *vis-à-vis* the problems and
needs of the least developed countries. The work of non-governmental
organisations has been very effective both in mobilising public opinion in
the developed world to respond favourably to the poorest countries, and in
ensuring that assistance reaches the neediest and more vulnerable groups
within the least developed world itself. We, in UNCTAD, count very much
on the work and co-operation of non-government organisations to meet the
challenge we confront.

Chapter 3

European Community Policy and the Poorest of the Third World

Maurice Foley, Deputy Director-General for Development,
European Community

The issue of how we respond to the needs of the poorest of the Third World
is one of the most important issues in the development debate. The whole
question of development is not about techniques, it is about how you respect
human dignity in all parts of the world. The EC comprises ten Member
Countries, including Britain, and they have formulated a common development
policy. Individual countries pursue their own development policy and the
EC common development policy is complementary, and of course it goes beyond
aid. The EEC of the Six was essentially founded by the French and the
Germans who were determined once and for all to pool their sovereignty, and
never go to war again against each other. Britain at that time decided
against membership. In 1973 when Britain joined there was already a
development policy. It was known as the YAOUNDE-Convention signed in the
capital of the Cameroons and it was formulated in the 50s, to take care of
the then colonies moving to independence, primarily France's overseas
territories, and Somalia, proposed by Italy was also included.

At the time of Britain's negotiations for entry, after consideration of
various options, it was decided to offer the Commonwealth countries in
Africa, the Caribbean and the Pacific, the same arrangements as were then
in existence if they so wished. A political decision was therefore taken
to deny these arrangements to the Asian sub-continent commonwealth countries,
presumably because they were too big, too impoverished, and too populous.
The result of the negotiations was the Lomé Convention, which involves the
whole of independent Black Africa with the exclusion of Angola and
Mozambique, who nevertheless are involved in some of these activities, and
will join in the next negotiations. Lomé is the centre-piece of development
policies of the Community, although resources are also made available for
the poorer countries of the world, for example development projects in Asia
and Latin America, and in sectors where there is real poverty. In addition,
there is an emergency aid programme and a major food-aid programme. The
whole programme added together is of the order of some two billion dollars
per year, which represents a considerable effort. This is administered by
the Commission, and of course the Member-States through the Council, and
the Parliament through its elected representatives, have their say in
formulating policy.

An important feature of Lomé is that it respects the concept of development

21

underlying aid and trade. It is not a charitable handout, but a genuine
effort designed to help people to discover themselves and their own
resources and to put them to the best use in the interests of their people.
An important problem for the poorest of the poor arises with what one
might call single commodity countries, for example where their whole
economy depends on production of coffee or cocoa. A fall in their basic
commodity prices on the world market has been accompanied by indifference
and selfishness of the developed world. As the prices of their export
commodity goes down, their purchasing power goes down, goods are unobtain-
able and their economies decline further.

Other poorest countries have very little to sell to the outside world.
Theirs is a question of survival. The question we have to ask ourselves
in the rich countries is what access do we give them to our markets? Behind
the anonymity of the Ten Member States of the European Community, two
countries can be reactionary and prevent anything happening and therefore
prevent an enlightened aid-policy and trade-policy. Often aid is the
palliative to a reactionary trade policy. When the poorest countries sit
down each year within the contractual framework of ministers and of member
states, they ask why are you giving us this money on the one hand and
denying us access to your markets on the other? It is a contradiction and
everybody agrees, but then we go away and nothing happens.

The poorest countries in ACP receive aid in a treaty arrangement under Lomé,
some between 20 and 100 million dollars over 4 to 5 years. They have
possibly an Ambassador and a small technical team in Brussels, working
directly with the European Community secretariat and the EC have in their
country a similar technical team, usually a small team of four or five, to
help get their projects off the ground. For the poorest of the poor we
have to move from what has been the heyday for the development theorists,
and for the business communities, and for the consultants. The shelves
of Ministers of Finance and Prime Ministers are full of studies paid for
out of development aid money, but which have never been read or never put
into practice. We face the problem of how to help them to spend the money
which is theirs on relevant projects, and this does not mean big prestige
projects of hydroelectric dams and major motorways but rather feeder roads,
storage facilities, subsidised fertiliser imports, and training at a local
level. Also important is quick action on lines of credit for on-lending to
small or medium-sized firms. The appropriate response to the poorest of
the poor is to reach them quickly, with no nonsense of feasibility studies,
and elaborate examinations, and visiting professors and missions from one
country after another, but quick action and a quick disbursement of the
money. Possibly the most immediate way that we can respond to the needs of
the poorest is by creating a petty-cash account for their disposal. There
has got to be accountability, and some degree of supervision in some
countries more than others, but we must avoid getting bogged down in the
rhetoric of development feasibility studies and technical assistance at the
cost of hundreds of thousands of dollars per year. In most of the poorest
countries the crucial issues are development of agriculture, diminishing
their dependency on food imports, and action to alleviate drought.

As part of the Lomé treaty arrangement the EC have a ministerial meeting
each year. We also have regular meetings out in the field, together with
our member-states and ministers from overseas, to create an effective
political dialogue and discussion. At such meetings the inconsistencies in
development policies become apparent. It is then that countries like the
Ivory Coast and Ghana who produce cocoa discover that the countries with
whom they are under contractual relationship, that is the countries of the

Ten, voted against their wishes with the other cocoa producers about
stabilising its price. So here you have an inbuilt contradiction: offering
with one hand a potential, and denying it with the other. This leads me to
conclude that the issue we are talking about fundamentally is not an
economic one, it is a moral problem. It is a question as to whether we
have a concept of man and his dignity; it is a question as to whether we
are concerned that in the environment in which he lives he can discover
himself, that he can be master of his own environment. Without that moral
influence we will simply play around between political parties arguing
together, but not taking strong effective action because there are no votes
in it. At the end of the day the man who believes in the Third-World, in
his own community, he is a dreamy idealist, and he is not in this world.

Some guidance for our response to the poorest may be derived from examining
those countries which have been more successful in helping the poorest.
I have lived in Brussels for 10 years almost, and the advantage of tele-
vision in Europe is that in Brussels you can get three Dutch programmes, and
three from Germany, Luxembourg and France, and if you are down on the coast
you can even get British TV. Then it is possible to see the extent to which
there is a policy of public education. For example, the Dutch can give
1 per cent of their GNP per year because they have educated their population
to understand the world in which they live, that for some it is a moral
interest, and for others it is a political one. If that tiny little nation
- the Dutch - can succeed, why cannot this country with all its history, its
resources and its links with the world outside? You can walk down the
streets in Britain and rub shoulders with people born in every part of the
world. Does anything rub off or is the reaction indifference? Politicians
will move when public indignation makes them move and that public indignation is a question of conscience. When we are considering the response to
the poorest of the Third World we are not examining economic niceties or
political niceties, but fundamentally a moral problem. What kind of a
world do we want to live in, and what kind of society do we want to see in
our own country and elsewhere? When I was appointed as Commissioner of race
relations - it was the first appointment made - I had a delegation from my
constituency who came to see me and asked me to give it up because I would
lose my seat. That was a measure of the degree and the depths of feeling.
There may not be the same degree of tension that there was in the early 60s,
but there are still major problems in the great cities of Britain. If we
cannot at home embrace this concept of respect with people whose skin is a
different colour, how can we be expected to reach out beyond our country
elsewhere.

It is a profound moral challenge for each of us in our own life, as to our
attitude to people who come to live in our own country, and of people overseas whom we shall never meet, but for whom as members of the human race we
have an obligation one to another. The question of our response to the
poorest nations in the world is similar to our response to the poorest in
our own country. If we are successful at home then possibly we will reach
out from that to think of others. We live in a world with extreme
imbalances of wealth and of poverty. Our politicians can plead poverty at
home but, compared with the drought and the horrors in the poorest countries
of Asia and Africa, our life is paradise. The question is one of the
concept of man, his dignity, and his destiny, and this should be the moral
imperative in making us make the effort and sacrifice to respond to the
needs of the world outside.

Chapter 4

British Government Policy and the Poorest of the Third World

Timothy Eggar, M.P., Parliamentary Private Secretary to the Minister of Overseas Development

All members of parliament know there is a committed, vocal and influential aid lobby but we must not deceive ourselves, since in fact more people in Britain are against than for aid. Almost any M.P.s postbag bears this out, however regrettable it may be, and public opinion, as well as the underlying economic situation inevitably puts restraints on development and aid policy. Lobbyists must protect the credibility of their case and our mutual cause by not becoming blinded by their own enthusiasm.

Every British government since 1929 has been in favour of overseas aid, and all political parties still speak in harmony on this basic principle - but we do have differing priorities within the aid programme as well as about the total level of expenditure on aid. Our government has had to act against a difficult economic backdrop. We have sought − and we now believe we have got - even greater value out of our overseas aid programme - both for the developing countries as recipients - and for us as donors. Of course the government is involved in overseas development primarily for humanitarian and moral reasons. Those who believe in liberty, human rights and common decency, must do what they can to help the less fortunate. But our motivation includes self interest, and we should not be ashamed of that; we are, above all, a trading nation. We rely for our prosperity on a market for our goods and the Third World represents vast potential markets.

It is worth stressing that the government's official aid is substantial - at £1028 million gross in 1982. In 1981, only five other countries (the USA, Japan, West Germany, France and Saudi Arabia) gave more than us despite our economic circumstances. This is equivalent to 0.44 per cent of our GNP - compared to the average among OECD donors of 0.35 per cent. The Chancellor announced that net aid in 1983 is to go up by 8.9 per cent on the net cash figure - giving a gross aid programme of £1105 million. With 5 per cent inflation predicted, that means a real increase in value - a considerable achievement at a time of economic stringency. We continue to concentrate our aid on the poorest countries - they got 68 per cent of our bilateral country aid in 1981 - better than most other donors and considerably more than the 1978 figure. This concentration on the poorest makes sense and is, I believe, welcomed by all. All official aid has to be justified on developmental grounds. Alongside our developmental objectives, we also

consider political, commercial and industrial factors. The key word is
"Alongside."

The government's aid policy brings protests - not from the Third World - but
from the British aid lobby. They are exercised that our aid might not be -
in their word - "real." I will try to deal with some of the specific
criticisms. The first is that aid is "political." Government aid is given
for many reasons - honourable and compatible reasons - without in any way
diminishing its developmental quality or benefit. Governments are heavily
influenced by their political and historical friendships, three quarters of
our bilateral aid goes to Commonwealth countries. We do not give bilateral
aid to Cuba or Vietnam because of their expensive military adventures in
other countries; we do not aid occupied Afghanistan. Our choice of recipients coincides with our political priorities. But since we give aid to 130
countries - including some with whose governments we have little ideology in
common - this means we have very open minds. Much of our aid - up to 40 per
cent this year possibly - goes through multilateral agencies where we - as a
single donor - have no veto. Sometimes we have to regard our membership of
these bodies as being more important than our distaste for particular
allocations of their aid. There is nothing new in this.

The second criticism is that the aid is commercially orientated. There is
nothing new, unique or shaming in a donor seeking commercial benefits from
its own aid. Less than half our aid is "tied" so that it is conditional
upon the purchase of British goods and services. We have to recognise the
political realities. Which taxpayers would support an aid programme which
paid for foreign tractors while British workers making similar tractors were
unemployed? The Aid Trade Provision is the 8 per cent of our bilateral aid
used specifically to help win export orders for Britain. A project has to
be developmentally sound and of benefit to the developing country. We use
the same appraisal criteria and techniques for all other aid proposals. Our
overseas competitors started to use an aid element which came to be known as
credit mixte export deals, and it was decided that Britain should do like-
wise. It was a scheme born of necessity, and orders - and jobs - have come
to Britain as a result. Since April, 1979, commitments of £139 million of
aid money have helped Britain to win orders worth £626 million. We are
unhappy about this spiralling credit mixte race which no one can afford to
win. Now there are efforts to introduce voluntary restraint and openness to
the practice, which we welcome.

The third major criticism is the way in which our aid is channelled and
particularly that it does not go to assist the poorest. In fact two thirds
of our bilateral aid goes to the poorest countries, and two thirds of our
multilateral aid also goes to the poorest countries, in total about £700
million in 1982. We fund projects and programmes to benefit the poorest
people in those poorest countries, and it is "good and real" aid by anyone's
definition, as illustrated by the following examples, selected from many.
In Egypt we have a mother and child health project costing over £4 million.
Our aid for capital projects in India usually grabs the headlines; yet there
we have given £35 million for small farmer lending and £15 million for 100
low cost housing schemes for a quarter of a million people. In Indonesia,
we are supplying over 60 tubewells; in Kenya, our projects cover rice
growing, cattle dips, husbandry training, afforestation, education aid and
agricultural development. In Lesotho, we have a £1 million woodlot scheme -
a £1.6 million agricultural training and extension scheme - and an arable
area conservation project. We've built four district outpatient clinics,
and provided workshops giving jobs to 270 people. In Nepal, we have an
integrated rural development programme costing £6 million. In Bangladesh we

are making available £17 million for an irrigation system which will provide 4,000 tubewells assisting 300,000 families.

ODA has over 1000 projects and programmes on the go at any one time. Many we fund by ourselves. An increasing number are co-funded with international agencies. The government also co-finances British charities on a "pound for pound" basis on certain projects, mostly aimed at the poorest. There were over 300 of these in 1981, double the level in 1980. There are ceilings on the "pound for pound" scheme. The obvious one is logistical, and yet another is that many agencies do not wish to be swamped by government money; they want to preserve their independence. The ODA projects which seem to "worry" the lobby tend to be the larger ones. These are intended to provide infra-structure or to increase national wealth - such as a power station, or port, or road system. They are of a size where only large national donors or multilateral agencies can take them on. They may not seem to benefit the poorest people directly; but they do provide the basic infrastructure which is a precondition to agricultural and industrial improvement. For example, we are spending about £40 million on the first all weather highway into Southern Tanzania; the poor farmers will at last gain access to markets. In Cairo, we are giving £50 million towards sewerage; a city with 11 million poor people will be freer of street sewage and disease. In the Sudan, £70 million provides generating equipment; with reliable power, large and cottage industry can grow and, as a bonus, there will be power to irrigate dry but fertile land.

A greater amount of local lower unit cost aid which is generally supposed to help the poorest, does bring its own particular problems. Such projects tend to be relatively cheap and slow-spending, and enormous amounts of government aid just could not be effectively spent. Despite their size, such projects can be as political as super-prestige projects. They affect the lives of people, for example, providing a well for a village can alter a local power structure or social pattern; it can create inequalities between villages that have and those that do not have wells; this is often dangerous ground. A large new rush of poverty focused projects would, in most countries, be out of the question in management terms. Dependence upon expatriate skills to launch and run such schemes can be counter-productive; but enough trained local manpower just does not exist. Building up national institutions can be a necessary preliminary stage.

The biggest driving force towards development remains as it always has been - determination and political will within the recipient country itself that the lot of its people will be bettered. As a government, most of our aid is on government to government basis. We have to be careful since we cannot interfere in the internal affairs of sovereign countries. If they want projects specifically for their poor, we will try to provide them. If they want dams, roads, power stations - we will try to help, provided of course they meet our development criteria. It would be very neo-colonialist of us to give only such aid as we considered to be good for their people.

There is no one "right" path towards development. Each developing country must be free to decide how they wish to develop and donors should respond flexibly. Donors provide individual contributions to a nation's development jigsaw - who finances what at any particular stage is less important than that the picture is ultimately complete. We do not pretend for one moment that we have got the balance between the conflicting aims and pressures within the aid budget absolutely right, however we do believe that we are respected worldwide both for the "quality" of our aid and for the size of our aid commitment.

Chapter 5

Our Response to the Poorest of the Third World – An Opposition Point of View

Kevin McNamara, Labour M.P. for Kingston-upon-Hull, Central

While there is a role to be played by voluntary organisations in assisting development of the poorest of the Third World, and indeed a role to be played by private capital, nevertheless the main thrust in achieving major improvements has to be by bilateral arrangements, nation to nation, and more probably multilateral co-operation, consortia of nations acting on an *ad hoc* basis, or through some of the international organisations. This is so primarily because voluntary organisations, despite dedication, skill and training of their members, cannot harness the organisation, finance and expertise necessary for large capital projects nor would they expect to do so. Secondly, private capital is not going to help the poorest of the poor, because private capital outflows go to where there is a return made on the capital and that is neither in the slums of Calcutta nor in the bush of Central Africa. There is no profit to be made there. And if one, in fact, examines those outflows of private capital flows they are going to the middle-income developing countries, or to those of the least developed countries which have a particular product which is marketable in the West and is capable of making a great deal of profit for the investors, whether it is a large company like Rio Tinto Zinc in Namibia or smaller companies which are, perhaps, dealing with commodities like farm kernel. Basically private investment can have little return in the poorest countries, and certainly the history of it since this government has released control for outflow of capital has been that while it may have gone to poorer countries, it has not gone to where the real problem is.

The policy of the last Labour government was aimed specifically to help the poorest of the poor in the poorest countries. For example, from 1975 the policy was implemented of giving grants rather than loans to the poorest countries and in July, 1978 loan repayments on outstanding debts from 17 of the poorest countries were cancelled. Now one cannot pretend that this was enough and as Chairman of the Select Committee of that time I was urging my government to do more, but, in fact, it was an indication of the right way forward at equally difficult times as those faced by the present government. Spending on overseas development rose from 0.37 per cent to 0.51 per cent of GNP over the period 1974 to 1979 and that was in terms of official aid loans. Despite the importance of private capital investment, what is needed is official aid on a government to government basis. Whilst we cannot dictate to sovereign Governments what their priorities are, we can in fact say what we are prepared to see our money spent on. However with the appearance of this present government the emphasis of aid policy was switched to trade, political, and defence criteria, all of which switched the emphasis both from areas of the poorest of the poor to areas which were politically sensitive and to areas where, with careful thought, we may not perhaps have wanted to see our money invested. For example, money has been sent to Pakistan but not for reasons of helping the poor of Pakistan but to provide a bulwark against the USSR advancement from Afghanistan. In fact under this particular government we have seen an abandonment of the concept of the .7 per cent GNP target for official aid. We have also had during the period of this government a general downgrading of the role of over-seas development being seen as something worthwhile in itself. First we had the positive downgrading of the overseas development ministry to an overseas development administration within the Foreign Office and the subordination of policy to Foreign Office considerations. Secondly we have had the disappearance of the skilled cadres of people employed within the overseas development administration, partly in privatisation, partly cutting down of staff, and by getting rid of them altogether, and of important institutions which have existed for the benefit of world development. Further we have had for the first time a Prime Minister who in fact has thought in terms of development aid as hand-outs, reflecting concepts and ideas which have swept the Western World over the past 5/6 years, and which was found in the tardy response of govern-ment to the Brandt committee report. It was the pressure of the Churches, and the pressure of the House of Commons Select Committee on Overseas Development that forced the government to look at the problems raised by Brandt. It was tardiness on the part of government that in the preparations for the Conference at CANCUN, British Government was not even represented, not because they would not have been welcome, but because they could not be concerned enough to want to go. I do not believe that foreign aid is politically unpopular. The forces that were harnessed not only for the lobby of Parliament but at hundreds of meetings up and down the country in village halls and in town houses, and every place that one went, reflected a concern and an interest in Brandt. There is an enormous sense of disappointment that at Melbourne, and at Cancun, nothin really positive came out of it, and the whole initiative seems to be bogged down in procedures and in rhetoric.

The Labour Party 1982 Programme passed by Conference detailed 17 points regarded as essential for the development of an adequate overseas aid policy. Although we say that this is a contribution that the UK can make to the problem of overseas development, it is something which only touches the fringes of the problems and what is needed is a concertive effort by the industrialised countries of the North. That does not only mean the Western democracies but also those countries that are engaged in Comecon. Indeed, the eastern block countries have a lot to answer for because of the situation that exists in the Third World. The biggest exporters of arms to Africa are in fact the Comecon countries, and they are also the smallest aid donors. I make the observation not to make a particular coldwar Margaret Thatcherish sort of statement, but because it is a fact. It is not just the western industrial countries that must give something, it is also the whole of the industrialised north.

There are two points in the Labour Party Programme which are specifically relevant to our response to the poorest of the Third World. Firstly, to achieve the United Nations target of official development assistance of 0.7 per cent of gross national product by the end of the first full parlia-ment, and thereafter to work towards a target of 1 per cent of GNP.

Secondly, to re-establish the principle that aid is to be used to attack poverty and hence should go first and foremost to the poorest people in the poorest countries. Given that women form a disproportionate percentage of the poorest of the poor both in rural and urban areas specific considera- tion will be given to their needs. Regarding allocation of bilateral aid, we will ensure that aid-funded products are in line with these objectives. Preference will be given to Governments which are carrying out policies which benefit the poorest, such as land reform, have a good human rights record, and respect trade union rights. In the case of countries who do not meet these criteria, Labour will attempt to help the poor by financing the particular projects of interest to poor people or by supporting independent organisations engaged in lifting the burden of poverty and oppression.

There are two additional points. First, on the international scene, and then on the domestic, which are of fundamental importance in seeking to tackle this problem. What often distresses many has been what has so often appeared to be an eyeball to eyeball confrontation over the interpretation of the North/South dialogues, the confrontation scenario rather than co-operation. This has frustrated the dialogue between the parties and the areas of mutual interest, however large or small between the North and South, have been lost in the rhetoric between the two groups, who have a variety of motives. Some are more concerned in scoring political points rather than any positive achievements. "The value of the arguments were never heard above the grinding of the axes." To compound this frustration, this dialogue with the deaf, the actual forum in which international discussions take place, often seems to be designed to hinder rather than help the painful discovery of areas of accord particularly the group system of bargaining in the United Nations. The Commonwealth Secretariat in "The North/South Dialogue: Making it Work", has produced a most valuable report by a Commonwealth Group of experts on overcoming the obstacles in the North/South negotiating process. The next Labour Government will seek to implement their many practical proposals to break the log jam of negotiating procedures, to overcome the mutual suspicions, and to channel the rhetoric in a more constructive manner, so that these impasses may be overcome.

If we are to succeed in this country in helping the poorest of the poor in the Third World, then we have to convince our own electorate that we have this degree of mutuality, this degree of self-interest, this degree of a shared human dignity. No government, whether it is a Labour government or a Tory government can progress in contributing to overseas development unless we can take the population along with us. This is most difficult in times of recession, and yet if the recession in our country is bad what are the effects of it in the Third World. For us it is the dole, but for them it is starvation and death. There is a real need for us to convince our own electorate of the reality of interdependence, of the need for planned trade between the North and the South, of the need to develop an open market, and to persuade governments of the necessity of having proper adjustment policies both in the North and in the South. A former Labour minister who has now become a Merchant Banker - and left the party, in front of the Select Committee was asked why does your department not have proper adjustment policies. He replied that in periods of expansion we don't need them, and in periods of recession we are afraid to have them. The non- government agencies can play their most important educative role using their experience gained in the field, and in the working of projects. Whether it is a missionary priest preaching on Sunday, or whether it is somebody from OXFAM speaking at a local women's institute, there is need to

persuade people of what can be done. It is a duty upon politicians to be
able to harness the sense of duty and compassion, that there is within
people, in order that they are prepared not only to make a one-off gesture
for Cambodian Refugees, or for the boat people, or for Solidarity in
Poland, but for a willingness, and a sustained willingness, to contribute
in the way it hurts the most, through their taxes.

In summary, the following areas are most important in the Oppositions view
to ensure an effective response of our society to the poorest of the Third
World:

1. The absolute commitment of the next Labour Government, both to increase
    the amount of money in overseas aid and to help to alter in absolute
    terms the quality of life of the poorest of the poor in the Third
    World.

2. The desire of the next Labour Government to identify and to eliminate
    those obstacles in procedures and forums which delay and frustrate the
    North/South dialogue.

3. A commitment to renewing development education, to restoring and
    increasing its budget in real terms so that we can convince the
    electorate and inform the world, not only of the desire, but of the
    necessity, in the terms of our self respect and human dignity, of
    helping the poorest of the poor in the Third World.

Chapter 6

Morality Plus National Interest

Sir Reay Geddes, a Deputy-Chairman of the Midland Bank

The following four working assumptions underlie an assessment of our
response to the poorest of the Third World for the medium term:

First, although Development means the all-round advancement of the
individual - it starts with simple economic provision: clean water,
food and shelter.

Secondly, the problems of poverty cannot be "solved" by political
shortcuts: least of all by mobilising one more UN voting bloc to
confront those whose help is sought.

Thirdly, it is not for us in business to think of creating a brave new
world, composed of new people, but to do our best in and around our
small corner of it as it is, and as it evolves - faster than is
usually recognised. We hope sovereignty will allow better international co-operation, but expect almost no supra-national control nor
an heroic Marshall Plan for Development nor global taxation.

Fourthly, both within a country and between countries the progress
of the poorest is closely bound up with that of the more fortunate.
The attack on poverty must be both direct and indirect: the latter by
increasing the general level of economic activity. This is best done
when governments provide an environment of incentives to encourage
individuals, families and companies to produce, think ahead and adjust
rather than by command and detailed central planning, with all the
lack of freedom, the tangled red tape and even corruption which can
follow.

What is the central problem? The poorest countries are those particularly
prone to some or all of these disadvantages: political insecurity,
misguided policies, weak administration, capricious enforcement of laws,
drought or floods, poor resources and rapidly growing population. A
combination of these limits very severely the growth of an enterprising
domestic commercial sector - stretching from the all-important small
family farmers and the workshop producers, who sell and buy in a nearby
market, to the travelling middlemen who so often provide a stimulus, to the
professions and on to the larger enterprises, public or private or mixed.

In this situation, the first charge on aid has to be essential consumption
to *alleviate* poverty so too little is left for human and physical infrastructure as a basis for directly productive investment, without which
no-one can hope to *eradicate* it. Foreign business, even if welcome and
fairly treated, has little scope to bring in productive resources. The
main burden of "priming the pump" for development rests on the over-
stretched national government, on grants or concessional aid and - thank
goodness for them - on the voluntary organisations.

Two more general questions should perhaps be touched briefly before we
come to the private sector itself. The first is this: would progress be
faster if priority were given to advance by Salients rather than spreading
scarce resources over even a moderately wide front? Without swallowing
whole the "take-off" theory, if those countries nearest to self-sustaining
growth were hurried through that barrier so as to stimulate exports and
attract capital and technology, could not still more of the available aid
be directed where it is needed most? The American Caribbean initiative may
at first have stumbled, but French concentration on a group of West African
countries shows what can be done and also how experienced administrators,
even from a former colonial power, can still be welcome and useful.
Zimbabwe has seemed to think along that line.

The second is this: it is not right that a country, once labelled
"Developing" should, as it progresses, remain so. The "graduation" of
countries should be expected and encouraged, as a matter of pride in
achievement, with changing relations between government and business and a
growing responsibility, first for their own poorest and then to a wider
community. "Graduation" can be seen in two-way investment, in expanding
South-South trade, and in the flow of aid from Opec countries. It can now
reasonably be expected of the Newly Industrialised in trade negotiations
and could, when appropriate, be negotiated into the conditions of loans
from inter-governmental institutions. This is how the International
Economic Order evolves, not by rhetoric, votes in the UN and decree. Thus,
a crucial issue is what, if anything, can be done by foreign business to
come in at an earlier stage of development than happens now?

The Scope of Foreign Business
To put the scope for foreign business into perspective, while private
foreign *loans* exceed official aid, the flow and influence of new *investment*
is relatively small, representing some 1 per cent of developing country GDP
(excluding Opec countries). As it is attracted by middle income countries,
the least developed get very little indeed. Yet, loans must be serviced,
while investment is only rewarded when profit is earned, and then the
operation sustains itself, typically "ploughing back" a good part of profit
after tax in new and improved activity.

We have to face some obvious but unpalatable facts. A business, like any
non-government organisation, is formed and operates thanks to a basic right:
freedom of association. Its purpose is to serve the needs and wants of
others and so to generate employment and create new wealth, which we accept,
not naively I hope, as a moral duty in a world of want. While proprietors,
partnerships or co-operatives can do as they will with their own, the joint
stock company, the main instrument, works under tight legal and fiduciary
constraints. In the first place, it is formed for stated purposes only,
with no power of general benevolence. It must compete to attract the
savings of others on trust to use them productively but prudently and to
reward those who entrust them. If well meaning directors use the funds for
other purposes they risk prison, and rightly so. They could hardly say in

a prospectus "part of your money will be for the general purpose of the business and part will be applied in countries of the highest risk, in projects unlikely to be viable and for charitable purposes."

The second constraint is that its first duty to all its stakeholders is to stay in business and do its chosen job even better. In stakeholders I include customers, suppliers, creditors and the tax gatherers. If the issue is seen simply in terms of shareholders and employees, with priority to the latter, these may lose customers and in time their jobs. In Britain, labour's share of income generated increased in the last decade from the low 60sper cent to almost 70 per cent at the expense of the corporate sector. As current failures and redundancies bear witness, it is really quite complex and difficult to get the balance right, so as to stay strong and secure through bad times, investing, innovating and training for the future. This is in part because the difference between profit and loss is so much smaller than the public believes. A recent survey in a number of European countries, including Britain, showed that public perceptions of profit margins are now ten times greater than the facts.

The third constraint is that the money available to the business is already committed to it: even a healthy bank balance is required for growth, innovation or against a rainy day. If there really were much more accumulating than was likely to be needed, it would surely be taxed away. So the idea, recently suggested, that large businesses should themselves create a sort of Marshall Plan fund for Development does not seem to be realistic.

Another constraint is the nature, or ethos, of the management. To succeed in competition typically requires the relentless pursuit of minor improve- ments in efficiency: saving a penny, a gramme or a second. Directors cannot require this of management but themselves behave like Lady Bountiful. Lastly, each business activity is highly specialised, even in a diversified group. This is illustrated by asking what mainstream activity and employment a major computer manufacturer, a petrochemical firm or a mass producer of cars could create just south of the Sahara, other than to offer good value as contractors or suppliers? Poor countries, too small for industrial diversification, find it very difficult to combine their markets for this purpose - witness the East African Federation.

But enough of the negative. The principal contribution of business, its mainstream operation, depends on the environment for enterprise which government creates. Given successful profitable operation, international companies can, and do try, to be "a good citizen" and do, selectively, willingly, but perhaps too quietly, support good causes and contribute to the work of those voluntary organisations who welcome that, for example, the ODI and IDS, the British Volunteer programme and British Executive Service Overseas. Financial institutions lend on a major scale to devel- oping countries for projects, for imports and exports, and to the World Bank, providing the greater part of its borrowing. Indeed, this year the Banks have been criticised as if they have been lending too much, at too great a risk. These are all valuable indirect contributions.

As well as doing their chosen business, companies also engage in community projects directly, all welcomed by host governments. As a few random examples, within my own limited knowledge, housing estates with schools, hospitals and sports grounds on remote sites; a circle of small-holders around a plantation, trained and helped by its management and integrated into rural development; a research and training project for small farmers;

the adoption of one or more villages some distance away from an industrial
complex; a proposed teacher training college; a British bank's fund for
promoting and financing what it calls "non-bankable" projects including
selected intermediate technology; community developments by consortium
investment banks; a programme developed by chambers of commerce jointly
with the International Trade Centre of UNCTAD and GATT, to improve the
competence of local chambers in export promotion and procedures for customs
and payments. One Latin American country, a few years back, asked its
leading chamber of commerce to run simple medical centres, to reduce the
waiting list at its hospital doors: that was successful. And so on. All
worthy contributions, not much publicised. Although the general rule is
that each specialist should literally "mind his own business" because he
probably does that best, there is still scope for initiative in joint
ventures with private sector companies as a catalyst, with only a modest
investment.

Can and should the private sector do more for the human and physical
infrastructure? It might be the concessionaire or partner or managing
agent of a national government in applying official funds, as the CDC does,
not only building projects but continuing as directors. It is worth
recalling that public utilities, transport and communications, as well as
agriculture and wholesale trade - import and export - were the first
sectors to be developed by what we now call "multinational" enterprise.
There used also to be privately run education, well respected. Political
fashion changed all that, but is it self-evident that this change has always
been in the true interest of poor countries? This line of thought may need
care: though the labourer is worthy of his hire, there is a reluctance to
link grants or concessional aid with continuing management fees and profit.
But with suitable safeguards, why not harness more often the problem-
solving and administrative ability of foreigners, including business
executives, bringing them in on appointment or secondment? It seems to fit
with current World Bank ideas for joint ventures with the IFC and might
apply to Regional Development Banks, the CDC and DCFC. The mechanisms do
exist.

In considering all this, the business sector welcomes the signs of a change
in the academic attitude towards multinationality. This used to be
concerned almost entirely with its *qualitative* aspects (influence, accountability, transparency, social impact and general conduct, with a dedicated
search for beams and motes in our eyes). All a necessary subject, if
sometimes overdone and leading to "guilt by association," and not my task
in this contribution. Now there is growing interest in the *quantitative*
aspects, asking what obstacles there are to a greater contribution to
development, sector by sector. Similarly, the annual report of the International Institute of Environmental Development foreshadows a programme to
relate the private sector to its work, for we should all be concerned to
ensure the sustained abundance of our planet - the true way to "subdue the
earth." If we are to bring "all hands to the pump" of development, such a
constructive approach to research, reflected in teaching, could help
today's practitioners and attract tomorrow's to a worthwhile and fascinating
career.

The Constituency for Development

Business people, with very few exceptions, have not been sure whether they
would be welcome and so have kept rather quiet. But there is, now, more
understanding of the role of business and wider acceptance of the fact that
both a country and a business enterprise can do well in its own interest

and do good for others at the same time: Brandt, Barbara Ward and the
Cancun Summit have accepted that one does not have to rob Peter to pay
Paul; as the saying goes, Development is not a zero sum game. This new
realism is spreading in developing countries, in international institutions and in many parts of the industrial world too, though not uniformly
because some people have still not come to terms with the way their country
earns its living. Those who work in multinational enterprises have equally
been learning what does promote Development and to understand better the
host countries' needs, aspirations and culture. So the time may have come
for them to consider whether policy and the official aid programme do fully
support Britain's national objectives, and more generally and openly to
associate their companies and employees with the Development Issues which
affect them. To carry conviction, they need to think and talk as a
practical "expert witness", not just a self-interested "lobby." I do not
suggest some general ecumenical effort with the many diverse and specialised interests in the World Development Movement, but only ask whether
there might be a more balanced influence on policy formation, supported by
a better informed public opinion, if this wider constituency were to join
hands at particular times on selected subjects.

Why is it, apart from the interest aroused by Brandt or a much publicised
Summit, that Development debates at Westminster are not better attended?
There seems to be a question whether aid does all reach and benefit those
for whom it is intended, while some see Third World development only as
exporting British jobs - despite an ILO study which refutes this. So aid
is constrained, while market access for imports is limited and outward
private capital flows are subject to constant demands for new selective
controls. Indeed interdependence, though inevitable, seems to be treated
as a concept to be resisted. Of course all this is immediately aggravated
by recession, but the condition is chronic. It may well be necessary for
weak sectors to seek and get subsidies or protection for a time but there
is no means of exposing the cost borne by the many against the benefit to
some, nor of ensuring that structural adjustment is indeed made and the
protection reduced at a careful but pre-determined rate. Neither the aid
lobby nor the trade lobby nor the consumer lobby can at present claim to be
very successful. But are they not natural allies, as trade provides
developing countries with much more essential foreign exchange than aid?

Mr. Evan Luard, from wide experience, has urged concentration on a very few
issues. Let us hope that this will be followed up. It might have been
"indebtedness" before the World Bank and Fund meetings, and "market access"
and "graduation" before GATT's meeting in November 1982. It might be
"commodity earnings" and "financial flows of all kinds" for UNCTAD VI, but
I am not sure whether the needs of the poorest should continue to be iso-
lated as a special subject, rather than stressed as an important aspect of
other subjects.

It may also be timely to re-think the underlying general appeal for World
Development. Over the years there have been many different voices: equity
and humanity, of course; but also "Brave New World" by edict; "look back
in anger" in colonial guilt; confrontation rather than common interest;
fear rather than hope and determination; denunciation rather than
encouragement; re-distribution of wealth rather than its creation, Third
World always right and having all the rights, so our countries always
wrong with all the obligations, and so on. Even if each is understandable
- have they all added up to a clear and persuasive call, likely to move
worried governments, harassed managers, anxious trade unionists and
preoccupied voters to do or support the right things?

Looking ahead, we know that, for Britain, jobs and real earnings and social provision all depend upon access to material supply and growing purchasing power of world markets. So Development is an essential national objective as much as a moral duty. The two do not contaminate but reinforce each other. Can we not blend more national economic interest with idealism, more efficiency with generosity, more recognition of what is done with the desire to do still better, and, above all, more concern for the future with our short-term self-absorption? That line of thought alone deserves an increased effort, by each interested party at World Development Education, if successive governments are to be supported in sound policy. And so to my final question: can we all, each in our own way and in our own circle, spread that message? Or, if not, why not?

Chapter 7

The Contribution of Trade Unions to the Poorest in the Third World

David Lea, OBE, Assistant General Secretary, TUC

"Workers and peasants, women and youth, organised in trade unions, cooperatives and other groups, will often be the guarantee of implementing reform in many social and economic areas. Such organisations can help in decentralising development activities, in mobilising resources particularly through self-help and public works projects and in providing social services, extension services, credit, and training inputs on a group basis."

This quotation from the Brandt Report emphasises the way in which Trade Unions, in all parts of the world where they are based on democratic principles, have a grass-roots credibility, which can be forgotten if we simply talk about world development in terms of macro-economics.

The approach of Trade Unions and the TUC to the desperate problems of the poorest of the Third World falls into two categories - and they are both based on the experience of the Trade Union Movement. First, we try to use our influence to press the decision-makers in the economic and social field on the need to adopt policies which will help rather than hinder the economic and social developments which alone offer real hope to the 800 million people in absolute poverty. Secondly, we use our experience directly, along with that of our colleagues in Trade Unions in the Third World - and we have very close relationships through our own international bodies - in the development of the sort of bodies which the Brandt Report referred to.

The Trade Unions were one of the first organisations to declare public support for the Brandt Commission report. We did not agree with every dot and comma but we do believe that the economic and political future of the developing countries and that of the industrial countries are very closely, if not inextricably, linked. There is no doubt that the expansionary policies and transfer of resources to the South, advocated by the Brandt Report, would provide at least a start in relieving the poverty of the Third World. We pressed this in debate which we instituted at the National Economic Development Council (NEDC) and we also insisted that the government reported back to NEDC on the Cancun Summit, as part of an on-going discussion. The outcome of Cancun was, of course, disappointing but we have to redouble our efforts.

We work closely with our colleagues in the International Trade Union
Movement for example, the European TUC, the International Confederation of
Free Trade Unions (ICFTU), the Trade Union Advisory Committee to the OECD,
and the Commonwealth TUC. We have extensive involvement with the ILO,
UNIDO and UNCTAD and make an important contribution to the United Nations'
Commission on Transnational Corporations. We endeavour, in all these
discussions, to put the priority on resources going to the areas most
relevant to the poorest in the Third World. Food and rural development,
health and education and training, energy requirements, transport and
housing. With our colleagues in the international trade union movement we
press for agreements that provide for basic human rights, rights set out in
the ILO declarations. The question is sometimes posed to the TUC - how can
you claim to support Third World Development when there is a groundswell of
trade union support for protecting particular industries? In response to
this a question may be posed in return. Why fundamentally has there been
a growth in protectionist sentiment? The problem of protectionism has
grown because of the slow-down of world employment. It has been recognised
for some time that rising unemployment leads to the growth of protectionism
and that is the way round the relationship goes. In trying to combat
protectionism, the real answer is to get world employment growing again,
and so the trend towards protectionism, and the reasons why there is a
growth in protectionism, will recede. World unemployment is a reflection
of an inadequate arrangement of our affairs in the world and, a tragic
waste of human and capital resources. There is a danger that we should all
now be trying to find scape-goats. The Japanese have just invented a new
English word called "scapegoatability." I am the First General Secretary
of the "International Union of Scapegoats." I think there is a danger that
we all try to blame somebody for a problem which is a problem that we all
have. The so-called world recession is not really an act of God, it is an
act of economic policy. In any event, free trade was also seen as an
unambiguous objective of economic and social policy. We do not see "free
trade", as a slogan, as being a slogan that reflects the total interests of
the Third World. We need many sorts of intervention, for example aid is an
intervention, which reflects the inadequacy of market forces.

We are all full of inhibitions about our own role and the role of our
organisations. Some will have inhibitions about discussing the link, which
the World Bank in its 1981 *Development Report* stressed, between the problem
of the poorest in the Third World and the issue of population growth and
pressure on resources. We all have to recognise our own inhibitions. It
is the task of Trade Unions to seek to improve living standards and ensure
employment and the satisfaction of basic needs of ordinary people and their
families. Trade Unions, therefore, are inevitably significant agents of
economic and social change. We can demonstrate that in all parts of the
world where there is an active Trade Union Movement, based on democratic
principles, you get a more equal distribution of income and wealth than in
countries that do not have an active Trade Union Movement.

Trade Unions in developed, as much as in developing countries, are also
important partners in helping to mobilise national resources behind
economic goals. Thus, the involvement of trade unions in the formulation
and implementation of development goals through a policy of national
consensus will help to ensure that there is popular support for official
policies. Without that support, or, particularly, against the active
opposition of the workforce, authorities will find the task of mobilising

national resources extremely difficult or even impossible. The relationship will not always be one of cooperation. Trade Unions will do
governments a service by telling them what is and what is not possible as
far as their membership is concerned. And that holds true of all countries
in the world. Sometimes it will mean that unions will feel bound to oppose
government policies and governments should listen if their policies are to
work.

Trade Unions, in Poland as in South Africa, in Chile as in South Korea are
among the main upholders of democratic freedoms and basic human rights.
Progressive churchmen, especially in the dictatorships of Central and South
America sometimes share the same platform. Such freedoms and rights are
important as an expression of human dignity. They are also essential to
the maintenance of a pluralistic society, and an advanced economic system
which is to serve the mass of the people. In countries like South Africa,
it is the Trade Unions who provide the only effective means for working
people to influence the decisions which directly affect them.

In view of these considerations it is not surprising that the best and most
direct way in which Trade Unions can help the poorest in the Third World
is, by helping them to build up their own organisations. The policy of
the TUC is, therefore, to provide practical help to incipient workers'
movements in the developing countries, especially in the area of education
and training. The TUC is held in the highest regard by Trade Union organisations in Commonwealth countries and other countries in the Third World;
a regard which is sometimes embarrassing when one meets it at first-hand.
The TUC has supported these organisations over the years in their struggles
for independence and we were always ready, within limited means, to provide
help in the development of effective, independent Trade Union organisations. We believe that the TUC still has a job to do. Our systems of
Trade Union education and training have a lot to offer. They are based on
our own experience in Britain, but we do help to develop organisational
skills which aim at creating self-reliance and that is just what is needed
among the Trade Union Organisations of developing countries in their own
relationships.

It has become common practice in many industrialised countries, for
governments to allocate public funds for Trade Union education and training
in the Third World. Such funding is normally agreed between the government
and the Trade Union organisation nationally, and it is required to meet
such costs as day-release, college fees, course development work and tutor-
training and it can run into millions of pounds. A central feature of such
state funding is, however, that the Unions are able to develop their own
programmes independently and decide on their own priorities. Overseas
assistance may involve the secondment of experts and skilled personnel and
the award of scholarships, for training abroad as well as the funding of
training within a particular country. In view of the growth of demand for
such assistance, overseas unions have looked towards their own governments
and inter-governmental organisations, such as the EEC, for funding. The
Commonwealth has placed greater emphasis on employment and labour issues
and in 1982, for the first time, convened a meeting of employment and
labour ministers and another meeting followed in 1983. These projects are
increasingly funded through official development channels.

Considerable amounts of official development funds for overseas assistance
are provided to national trade union bodies in, for example, the Nordic
countries, the Netherlands, West Germany, the United States, the Eastern-
bloc countries, and more recently Australia and Canada. We are aware of

the pitifully low level of public funding for development education in
Britain. In this country the amount of funding available for Trade Union
assistance overseas, currently £50,000 a year, has also been pitifully low.
One must compare it to literally millions of pounds made available in other
Western European countries, let alone the USA and the USSR. Whether or not
this is politics, one cannot ignore the tremendous expansion of the effort
being made by Moscow in this field. It is, therefore, the strong hope of
the TUC that the ODA will increase this amount so as to allow British
Unions to play their role - especially in Commonwealth countries, since we
have a special role in the Commonwealth.

The direct assistance activities of the TUC are only a small part of its
involvement in international work. We are the second biggest affiliate of
the International Confederation of Free Trade Unions and, of course, we are
the largest affiliate of the Commonwealth TUC. Both these organisations
provide massive training assistance but they also intervene to help Trade
Unionists who are victims of repression in so many developing countries.
I have visited the Philippines on the United Nations Commission for Transnational Corporations and while we were there, one of the members of the
delegation from the local centre was arrested. I was able to lead a delegation to the Foreign Minister which at least ensured, I think, that due
process of law was used in his trial. But that is one illustration amongst
thousands of illustrations of the fact that the Trade Union Movement is
often the ally of human rights development. With the support of the TUC -
financial as well as moral - we have provided funds for the defence of black
Trade Unionists in South Africa and we have supported the families of Trade
Union representatives in jail or detention for trying to do a trade union
job. We have co-ordinated the efforts of the independent Trade Union movement to influence the policies of the United Nations, and it is we who have
the accepted leadership role as opposed to the organisations who look
towards Moscow for their spiritual sustenance. In all its international
work the TUC defends Trade Union rights. This is essential in itself but it
is also a means of offering, as we see it, a key to political economic and
social development in the Third World. Unions are a potent force in
promoting respect for human rights, for achieving universal suffrage as well
as securing basic material needs. Trade Unions are, in this sense, engines
of development and should be seen in this light by all of those who wish to
see genuine development. We warmly encourage co-operation with all of the
churches. The Trade Union Movement around the world is divided in certain
ways along lines not entirely dissimilar from the division of the churches.
But we think a lot of progress is being made to find common policies and we
believe that in the future co-operation will develop.

Attention is often focused on the role of the Transnational Corporations in
transferring technology and development. It is equally important that
trade unions should do what we can to build bridges between North and
South. The Trade Union Movement is one of the few organisations, perhaps
the only organisation, with grass-roots credibility, that does have some
power to directly influence development in terms of the transfer of capital
in the on-going structures of the Transnational Corporations. Looking
ahead to the year 2000 - the role of Western capital in the economic
activity of the Third World is going to grow and not lessen. We should
therefore consider how far we can ensure that genuine representatives of
the work-force in all countries of the world can meet together through
bodies which relate to the particular Transnational Corporation in which
they happen to be employed. If we are to avoid tension between North and

South, institutions which have grass-roots credibility both in the North
and South should be encouraged. The Trade Union Movement will only be able
to act as a bridge, if the corporations themselves, in co-operation with
the UN, are able to avoid a polarisation between groups who perceive their
self-interest to be mutually opposed.

Chapter 8

The NGOs and the Poorest of the Third World

Sir Geoffrey Wilson, The Chairman of OXFAM

To get the issue in perspective we might ponder on how good we have been at helping the poorest in our own society. From the lady bountiful with her basket of goodies in the last century, to the poverty trap our present taxation system and the form-filling and queues of our social security offices, we are well-meaning, but often clumsy, unimaginative and insensitive in our modern welfare states. How much more difficult is it for us to try and help the poorest overseas - to put ourselves in their shoes (and even that metaphor assumes a level of prosperity that few enjoy) and see the world from their vantage point, rather than to sit in our Committees and prescribe programmes and solutions that too often turn out to be inappropriate and unsuccessful anyway.

The non-governmental organisations have long been in the vanguard of helping the poor. And the church is probably the oldest NGO of all. Alongside the sometimes inappropriate preaching of christianity and the wearing of clothing, the church missionaries set up schools and hospitals overseas, providing often the only educational and medical services in rural areas to this day, and working with the poorest in city shanties and slums. That tradition has widened and expanded over the years to include agriculture, vocational training, appropriate technology, many social programmes, and even the provision of legal aid services. Indeed, now that shorts and a shirt seem to have replaced the clerical collar in most overseas locations, spotting the priest is not always easy. You can be sure, however, that he's there with the poor, rather than wining and dining with the rich. The priest, or today's secular equivalent, the field worker, in working with the poor, and often living with them too, has the key to helping them. He or she knows their problems from the *inside*, but he also has the privilege of being an outsider with that extra dimension - a knowledge of the possibilities beyond their experience. He can open doors they never dreamed even existed in the enclosing walls of their poverty.

This local presence and local sensitivity is something very special to the voluntary agencies. No foreign government representatives and few UN experts can really get in there and work with the people. It is the non-political nature of the agencies that gives them the freedom to go where others cannot. We are privileged to enjoy this responsibility in many parts of the world.

Elsewhere, however, this freedom is at risk or restricted currently - in countries like Guatemala, El Salvador and Kampuchea. In such areas the work may be limited and restricted - by fighting, repression, or by government regulation. But local NGOs usually manage to continue to work, often under extremely difficult and sometimes dangerous circumstances. Getting help in from the outside can be difficult too. But the link with outside agencies and the friendship of our common humanity in the face of great suffering may be more important than any specific amount of aid funding.

Being non-political stretches a lot further than helping in Kampuchea and Guatemala where no British government aid programmes can go. Helping minorities, neglected by their own governments and sometimes looked down on by their fellow citizens, is a priority task for the NGOs. It may be specific groups like the Tamil tea estate workers in Sri Lanka, the tribal people in India, or the Amerindians of Brazil. Or it may be much larger groups like refugees, the disabled, or even the largest minority of all - the women - who get left out or overlooked by male legislators and civil servants the world over.

The type of assistance varies to meet the needs: to take the Tamils from Sri Lanka as an example, clean water supplies for the still dreadful housing in the estate "lines", and community centres with reading and recreational facilities on the tea estates. And for the Tamils who have opted to return to India many small local voluntary groups have assisted, together with outside agencies, providing creche facilities, vocational training, land purchase, house building materials, wells, and seeds, to supplement the loans allocated by the Indian government to each returning family. But perhaps the most important aid of all was the provision of funds for the salaries of a group of social workers to help the repatriates from the moment they arrived off the boats, through the jungle of land purchase or job seeking, learning how to grow food rather than tea, or to work in hot factories rather than on the cool hills. The story of that repatriation of some 390,000 people in the last 15 years remains to be written. I do not think anyone comes out of it very well, but at least the voluntary agencies tried to help some of those frightened stateless people returning "home" after one hundred and fifty years. No bilateral aid programmes or UN agencies were to be seen.

The Indian government has done much more to help its own minority tribal people, with programmes of land allocation and financial assistance, and the specially low preferential interest rate charged by all the banks to poor people. But most tribals are illiterate, and most live in remote rural areas. Consequently few of them know of the possibilities open and available to them, a problem that we face in our society with low uptake of some of the welfare benefits. There the voluntary agencies have helped by spreading the message; and in one area of India, paying for the training of barefoot legal/social workers. Or more precisely providing the wherewithal to run a service that is a cross between a rural citizens advice bureau and a free legal aid centre. Even more unlikely for a voluntary agency is the new role that has evolved over the last 10 years of providing bank collateral for the tribals and other poor groups to release loan funds from their own banks for them. Some Oxfam supporters might be unhappy to think of their donations sitting in an Indian bank. But if they then learn that this deposit has released 3, 4, or even 5 times as much in loans to the poor, they might recall the parable of the talents, and feel that their funds have been put to wise use.

Paying bus fares might also appear to be a doubtful use of funds. But

helping representatives of scattered Indian groups in Brazil to get together
from time to time, enables them to discuss their common problems, and work
out a common front in dealing with the Brazilian government, and the large
commercial interests that are encroaching on their forest homelands.

Another example of our "small is beautiful" role is the funding of travel
and accommodation costs for some Tanzanian provincial forestry staff to
visit some schools and villages who had started tree growing projects in
the neighbouring province - and they have now started similar programmes
back home. Another small enabling grant was a 5/- sprinkler for a hose for
a group of leprosy sufferers who were trying to grow their own vegetables
in Uganda, and £143 as an interest-free loan for the purchase of needles
and thread to employ 280 people in Bangladesh to make prayer caps for sale.
(80 per cent of the loan was repaid in under twelve months.)

Requests for aid on this scale would nonplus my erstwhile employers - the
Overseas Development Administration and the World Bank. Their systems
could not cope with bus fares, sprinklers, or needles and thread. Or if
they tried, it would have been 10,000 sprinklers, and British made. The
ability and experience of the voluntary agencies to work with small groups
who need small amounts of assistance is by far and away their most important contribution in the field of aid and development.

Flexibility is another key aspect of the operations of NGOs. Not only is
there a wide variety of aid-giving agencies - (and this can cause confusion
and difficulty to would-be aid recipients who do not know their way
around). But many of the agencies are free of constitutional and other
organisational difficulties, like the national quota systems that restrict
the recruitment of UN personnel, for example; and are free to help in the
way most appropriate to the situation. My own agency's experience in the
last few years illustrate these advantages. Oxfam is essentially a non-
operational agency. We do not recruit dozens of doctors, nurses, vets,
agriculturalists, engineers and so on to run our projects. We fund other
agencies and small local groups working in the field, responding to
requests and seeking out the needs through our system of field directors
and assistants around the world. For response to emergency situations,
however, we do "go operational" on occasion, calling on doctors, engineers
and others from our "disasters register" - a panel of people who are
prepared to go overseas at short notice for limited periods, recruited
during the course of the seventies. But even this group of useful people
could not meet all the needs and requirements that have poured into us, and
sometimes nearly *over* us, in the last few years. Engineers to install
water and sanitation for the boat people, refugee camps in Malaysia to
assist UNHCR. Doctors, nurses, water engineers and agriculturalists to
work with the refugees in Somalia. Nurses and doctors to reopen some of
the abandoned and damaged mission hospitals in Zimbabwe at the request of
the government. And a variety of skilled people to staff the team in
Kampuchea. We have had to expand our own staff at our headquarters to cope
with all these people - their health requirements, insurance, travel, etc.
Ten years ago we would have been horrified at the prospect. Perhaps in our
quieter moments, some of us still are, but we are not alone. Christian Aid
recruited a medical team to work in war-torn Lebanon, and a number of
European agencies, not normally operational, recruited specialists to work
on the Consortium team in Kampuchea.

Just one more example of "going operational" in a very different context.
Following the thesis "if you can't find anyone else to do it, do it your-
self," our Field Director in Upper Volta in West Africa several years ago

persuaded us to recruit a forestry expert and to start a project to grow
trees for firewood, using the principle of small micro-catchment planting
areas to catch and hold the rain water, similar to those he had seen on
holiday in Israel the previous year. The first forester appointed was a
woman, a former Peace Corp volunteer. The first thing she did was to
undertake a survey of village women to find out what firewood they used,
what they preferred, and why. To her and our delight, she uncovered a
wealth of wisdom - a veritable encyclopaedia of fuelwood knowledge. They
preferred bushes to trees - nearer the ground, so easier to cut, and more
quickly regenerating. They knew, in great detail, which wood was best for
kindling, for slow burning, in the wet, in the dry, at different seasons of
the year. An annotated list was drawn up with many species the professional
foresters knew nothing of. It has now passed into the teaching of the
Commonwealth Forestry Institute in Oxford. No-one has ever thought of
asking *women* before.

After the euphoria of this exploratory stage in the programme, the inevitable problems arose - the goats, the cost and therefore impossibility of
fencing, seedlings dying in the drought, and many others. But everyone
"hung on," and now 4 years later the programme has evolved with its own
local flavour. "The project's runoff techniques based on experiences in
Israel were completely metamorphosised when applied to the different
conditions found in the Yatenga ... still attempting to exploit runoff
water but now resembling traditional methods of erosion control - construc-
ting small rock dikes across areas subjected to excessive overland water
flow, laying bundles of dried sorghum stalks on the ground to serve the
same ends, and planting perennial grasses around fields." So wrote the
project director in 1982 reporting on the work, now in 30 villages. And
when Oxfam's current Field Director (not the project originator) wrote
recommending continuing funding for next year he concluded: "A project that
started as a technical solution has now blossomed into a social and
organisational one. The techniques have been integrated and adapted by
their users, so the key questions become those of promulgation. The fact
that Oxfam is now the leader in this field means that we have a responsibility to carry on, especially as it is the farmers themselves who are
proving that if the mix is right and if they are interested in what is
happening, tractors, food aid, and the like become irrelevant!"

This example is quoted at some length for several reasons. It shows a
flexibility of approach by Oxfam and exemplifies a flexibility and sensitivity of approach there in the Yatenga which has made the programme the
success it is in the villages. And it is a classic example of the development worker with one foot inside and one foot outside. Add the local
women to that recipe, and you have a good chance of success.

The project is also a good example of experimentation, another role that
the NGOs can often carry out more easily than government and larger bodies.
Work on solar water pumps, gobar gas plants, emergency housing, sanitation
units, and water kits - these are just some of the physical items that come
to mind. Perhaps more important are the human experiments. This term may
give the impression of human vivisection, but all development programmes
are to some extent experimental. I am thinking of some of the functional
literacy programmes designed and evolving to meet the needs of particular
localities - like the slum school in St. Martin, Port-au-Prince, in Haiti
where parents and housing co-operative members teach part-time, and the
children plan and discipline themselves. They learn straight reading and
arithmetic; but other subjects range over cleanliness and hygiene (so
difficult but so necessary in this sprawling shanty area), working together,

local geography and so on. Thousands of miles away in Bangladesh, more
than a thousand men and women are involved in an organisation initiated with
the help of Caritas in the mid seventies. Alongside a range of other
activities including vocational training and family planning, they have
developed a literacy programme based on 25 key works and 25 lesson sheets,
each representing a rural problem of the poor. By this means simple
literacy and awareness-raising have been combined, and high rates of attend-
ance even at the end of a working day testify to the popularity of this
scheme. No Ministry of Education would feel able or even be much good at
devising locally-orientated programmes like this. In the same way Ministries of Health may not always be the best devisers of training and programmes for paramedical workers. Not only are they middle class and city
orientated, but our Whitehall legacy of separate ministries does not always
suit local conditions: medical services come under Health, nutrition and
food under Agriculture, and clean water under Public Works.

So it has been fascinating to watch the many and varied programmes that have
been developing around the world over the last 10-15 years - paramedics in
Bangladesh, both men and women who apply for the job, receiving a year's
training, half at the centre, and half in the field - the brainchild of the
charismatic Dr. Zaffrulah Choudhury. By contrast the Aroles' programme in
Maharashtra in Western India is built on women village health workers who
are selected by their own villages, and are trained on-the-job with an
older experienced worker. Further south in Tamil Nadu the Kottar Social
Service Society, working without a doctor, has evolved an apparently
complex variety of personnel - health guides, health educators, village
health workers, and voluntary village extension workers. Over 90 per cent
of the local people participate in this programme, paying for the privilege
of doing so - a remarkable achievement in only 10 years. The various people
cover sanitation, vegetable growing, maternal and child health, and immuni-
sation, as well as providing a curative medical service. It cannot be
coincidence that this area has the highest female literacy rate in India.

Sharing experiences is important too. These schemes may each be just right
for their own locality, but there often are many lessons and problems that
can be shared. And so the voluntary agencies act as catalysts too - running
local workshops, workcamps, seminars - or enabling them to happen. Paying
those bus fares again! Or encouraging agencies to expand their programmes -
hospitals to undertake rural outreach, or more specialised agencies like the
West Bengal Spastics Society in Calcutta to extend its work out into the
rural areas; or to help a fishermen's organisation in N. E. Brazil expand
to reach more people and even to protest to the increasing number of
industrial units that are polluting the coastal waters there.

And so I come full circle and back home to the role of the voluntary agencies in the rich world. We in the United Kingdom are constrained by the
law and its watchdogs the Charity Commissioners. We cannot, as charities,
mount the protests or organise the lobbies that are deemed political under
the existing law. Our colleagues in many other countries are not so constrained, and can enter into more active dialogue with their legislators.
But whatever the freedoms or limitations, we all have a grave responsibility
to educate and make our fellow citizens aware of the needs of the poorest
among our fellow human beings. Indeed, President Nyerere of Tanzania has
charged us with that role as equal in importance to helping the poor
directly.

Sometimes we feel that our voices are small and unheard - a voice in the
awful wilderness of our own unemployment and other home problems. Some-

times, overseas, the small projects whose virtues I was extolling earlier
seem to be in danger of being swamped by mammoth programmes, rapacious
landlords, drought and many other threats and dangers. But if despair
threatens, it is heartening to remember that some 10,000 people turned up
at Westminster to lobby their MPs on the Brandt report; and that tens of
thousands of people in this country help the overseas aid voluntary agencies
with time and money every day. Another initiative we shall be watching
with interest and concern is the Channel 4, and especially the fortunes of
the International Broadcasting Trust set up by more than 60 voluntary
agencies to make and bring more programmes on Third World issues before the
public. This enterprise should help widen concern for the many and
various issues that relate to the poorest in the world.

As we battle against all the other conflicting interests, it is salutary
that we should remind ourselves that taxation and the redistribution of
wealth in our own societies is a relatively recent phenomenon, still
continuing, but now accepted as a fact of life. Perhaps it is not too much
of a dream to hope that the Brandt report's idea of a World Development
Fund - from a tax on armaments, or tourism or some other feature, is not too
far away. Meantime, may I conclude with Willy Brandt's own words - the
conclusion of his introduction to the report:

"The shaping of our Common future is much too important to be left to
governments and experts alone. Therefore, our appeal goes to youth, to
women's and labour movements; to political, intellectual and religious
leaders; to scientists and educators; to technicians and managers; to
members of the rural and business communities. May they all try to understand and to conduct their affairs in the light of this new challenge."

Chapter 9

The Poorest of the Third World – A Christian Concern

The Right Reverend R. Runcie, The Archbishop
of Canterbury

At first glance my addressing the issue of a "Christian Concern" for the
poorest of the Third World seems to give me considerable scope to indulge
myself in what a fellow bishop once called: "the fatal facility for
continuous utterance." Perhaps it is a particular trap for an Archbishop -
who is expected to be able to sound off on each and every subject: but who
has all too little time for the sort of reflection which produces thought
of a substance and depth which an issue of this importance deserves. There
is too much at stake to allow the fatal facility to rule, and I hope that
what I have to write will reach you not because it is being written by an
Archbishop, but because it is true and because it demands a response.

I would like to start with a brief word for those who say that Churchmen
should keep out of the political arena by pointing out what Christians have
achieved by getting involved. For example, in 1941, my predecessor as
Archbishop of Canterbury, William Temple, convened the Malvern Conference.
The purpose of that meeting was described as "to consider what are the
fundamental facts which are directly relevant to the new society that is
emerging and how Christian thought can be shaped to play a leading part in
reconstruction following the war" - an ambitious agenda - the sort of thing
which might be dubbed in the cliches of our own day "trendy rhetoric."

After the conference, Temple gathered around him at Lambeth a number of
leading economists and the book *Christianity and the Social Order* was
published. In that work, now of course somewhat dated, but rightly
influential at the time, Temple pointed out that religion must be concerned
with the total life of society, including economics and politics. To those
who accused him of stepping into highly technical matters, he replied that
as a Christian he had an obligation to support the cause of the under-
privileged and if they were to be supported, then this meant working for
economic reform.

That is an example from this country and from the past: but today we are
hearing its echoes in relation to our understanding of the world as a whole.
When I was at the World Bank I was told by Bob MacNamara, the President,
that he went to the Harvard Business School to deliver a lecture on the
Brandt Report - he told his audience that there were moral arguments, but
he would concentrate on what was likely to interest and influence them -

the arguments from mutual self interest. At the end he was severely taken to task by questioners who asked why he thought they were not interested in the plain moral case. Over the last few years, and particularly since the publication of the Brandt Report, the Churches and the development lobbies have gained a maturity and a professionalism which has been lacking in the past.   Those of us in positions of influence must cultivate this deepening awareness of the need for hard work as well as heart-stretching rhetoric.

Why should this realisation of Christian principle be applied to the world stage, and at this time? I think the answer to this lies in the concept of brotherhood, which I would argue is central to the Christian faith. In the battle against the Slave Trade, the 18th Century principle of individual human rights and the utilitarians' correction of that with the doctrine of the greatest good of the greatest number, played their parts, in this country a major inspiration came from evangelicals like Wilberforce, and their poster of a black man and the caption "I am a Man and a Brother." If you view the world from the understanding that all men and women are brothers and sisters - you find that the religious vision is now being substantiated by the way our world is developing. I can pick up my tele-phone in Lambeth Palace and talk to the Archbishop of Nigeria - or Japan, or Australia, or the Solomon Islands.

No great religion, least of all Christianity, has ever suggested that moral obligations begin and end with the citizens of one particular state at one particular time: and I find it heartening that there is, and especially among young people, a great and growing consciousness that the gross disparities between our own affluent, developed nations and those of the struggling southern hemisphere are not just a threat to our own, still rather cosy economic order. Our rising generation is the first to have grown up with a view of planet earth from the outside: the photographs of our beautiful planet, taken from outer space, are not, as perhaps they are to older generations, just symbols of technological advance. They show the world from beyond the artificial barriers which man in his ignorance and greed has created. They have lived with this vision of the world in its entirety and they have seen no reason why it should not be beautiful for all who dwell upon it.

Forty years later, the essential principle that Temple stood for has not changed. Those who would follow Christ are obliged to support the weak, the poor, and the deprived: in the words of Cardinal Hume, "We need to see the unbreakable connection between love of God and love of our neighbour." The establishment of this connection must lead to the conclusion that parallel to the pursuit of brotherhood is the pursuit of justice for *all* those embraced by the fatherhood of God and this brotherhood of man. This is a principle which, in the words of our time, is non-negotiable.

Have all those who call themselves Christians lived up to this ideal? The answer, of course, is No; but many *have* sacrificed their lives to the service of the less fortunate: and it is they who have done so in the past, and who are doing so today, who give me the moral authority to state, in their name, what we, as people of influence in our various fields, must do if we are to call ourselves Christians. We may not be called to follow particular examples of service in the field: but from wherever they are - from the islands of Indonesia to the mountains of Nepal, from the plains of Uganda to the forests of Brazil, they look to us to support their work: and they look for many kinds of support because there are many ways of demon-strating a Christian concern.

For many people, this may mean raising money through a Church jumble sale.
For others, it will mean running classes and discussion groups to arouse
greater public awareness of the work which needs to be done. For others
still, support will be mainly vocal. The mass lobby of Parliament on
5th May, 1981 which ensured that the subject of world development reached
the political agenda and could no longer be ignored by any serious politi-
cian, was due almost entirely to efforts by the Churches, and 80 per cent of
the people who supported that lobby were active Christians.

These activities at home, and the truly remarkable achievements of Christians working all over the world - often working in the most distressing and
dangerous conditions - give us the right to be heard on these issues. I
present the case not as a vague voice delivering a pocketful of rhetoric
from some ecclesiastical ivory tower: but as the proud representative of
many thousands who work to fulfil their obligations which carry Christian
labels - such as Christian Aid - but in more neutral agencies also - the
Save the Children Fund is an obvious example. Part of the obligation of
being a Christian is that of saying aloud what you believe to be right, and
I make no apologies for it. The admission of Christian concern must lead
to a proper study of the issues to which that concern is applied: Christians
must not allow themselves to be fobbed off by those who claim a monopoly of
technical knowledge, nor by those who simply refuse to listen. If we want
people to take us seriously we must ensure that we are properly prepared.
The Zulu chieftains had a favourite order of battle, known as the horns of
the buffalo because it involved launching a two-pronged attack on an enemy,
to take him in both flanks at once. The horns of the Christian buffalo are
those of sound knowledge and clear moral authority.

I would like now to look at the implications of Christian concern for
official policy towards the developing nations. We are all aware of the
problems of our own Western economies, and that the resolution of our
economies will do much to assist those of developing countries. I am glad
that in a very difficult economic situation the Government has not resorted
to the kind of siege mentality, restrictions on overseas investment and
import quotas which would further damage the international economy.
Resisting demands for protectionism is extremely important to Third World
countries; and for the wealthier of the developing countries in particular,
private finance and investment has a vital role to play. By 1980 private
flows from Britain to developing countries totalled £4,800 million.
Combined official and private flows for that year were about £5½ billion or
about 2.5 per cent of our Gross National Product. This is well above the
United Nations target figure of 1 per cent - this is pleasing and it is to
be regretted that we cannot meet the other main target, that of 0.7 per
cent of Gross National Product for official development assistance. There
are, I am assured, good *technical* reasons for the fall in Britain's official
aid performance - from 0.52 per cent of Gross National Product in 1979 to
0.34 per cent in 1980. We should also be doing ourselves an injustice if
we were to ignore our trade flows, which are some twenty times larger than
official aid flows. I apologise for quoting statistics at length, and I
am fearful of joining what the Minister for Overseas Development has called
the "pocket calculator brigade", but they form an important background to
the increasing concern which many in development work have voiced to me
about present attitudes to development issues, and the whole way in which
the matter of official aid is being approached.

One of the present government's much quoted intentions in the development
field is "to give greater weight in the allocation of aid to political,
industrial and commercial considerations alongside basic development

objectives." There is much debate about how effective government to government aid can be under certain circumstances, and I admit that I have seen
some of the dangers at first hand in Africa and Asia, but aid tied to
commercial or political considerations will inevitably be constrained by
exactly those considerations. It is obviously vital that British firms win
foreign orders and contracts: and sometimes they may need government assistance in order to do so. But in my view it would be absolutely wrong were
that assistance in any form whatsoever to be taken out of the aid budget.
Doubtless the country so assisted benefits: but where assistance is given
partly in order to preserve jobs here at home: effectively a form of
government subsidy: then the funds should come from the Department of
Industry, not from the Overseas Development Administration. We must insist
that funds earmarked for genuine development purposes are not swallowed up
in disguised subsidies. Trade and aid even when they serve the same
ultimate purpose are two different matters and they must not be confused.
Of course trade is vital and of course constructive trade assists development - but perhaps we have become over-obsessed with development at the
expense of basic humanitarian aid. This possibility was brought home to me
by one aid worker who is concerned particularly with government funding of
health and welfare projects: he said: "The idea of welfare for its own sake
has gone out of the window. It's development or nowt."

I sense a real crisis of confidence among those who work in the development
field. Not only do they feel hamstrung by the lack of resources, but they
feel that they must battle constantly against official lack of support.
The Government will protest that this is not the case, and that it is
genuinely and wholeheartedly committed to world development. The point I
must make however is that the standard bearers in the aid agencies *do feel*
deserted - that their support has dwindled to nothing and even gone into
reverse. The Government figures may counter this view, but moral support
is always as vital as material support: and you can cut off that moral
support either directly - by restraining your commitment to aid - or indirectly by - for instance, phasing out all government funding for development
education. The withdrawal of funds from the Centre for World Development
Education from 1984 - is a particularly sad case - yet another example of a
small organisation which, if it does not just close down, will have to
expend valuable time and energy on fund-raising. If a government makes
these kind of cuts it takes more than rhetoric to restore lost time, lost
programmes, lost effort and lost confidence. The Churches' involvement in
development education is very considerable, so I can speak about it with
the confidence which comes from belonging to an institution with a relatively clear conscience.

There are a number of steps which might rectify these growing suspicions of
official indifference. There is an overall need for the government to
express its commitment to the poorer nations without throwing up at the
same time a smokescreen of caveats and qualifications. That commitment
might well be clearer, for example, if the Minister for Overseas Development
was in the Cabinet - not a purely cosmetic change - but so that he may
defend and support the aid vote in times of financial stringency. I have
already noted the need to support development education in order to
achieve greater public acceptance for overseas aid, and I look forward to
the day when, through the efforts of those who seek to arouse the public
conscience, overseas aid becomes an election issue. It is already the case
in the Netherlands and perhaps other places in Western Europe. I feel that
day may be nearer than some politicians seem to realise: and the government
would do well to look again at the conclusions of the Report of the all-
party Foreign Affairs Committee which was published in July, 1982, and to

re-think the response to them, especially where they relate to development education.

But I have a still more fundamental concern yet, and this is that we - as a society, represented by our government - have yet to take on board the enormity of the developing world's problems. There are some figures which are simply too large to be entered on the screen of the average pocket calculator. The 800 odd million people, for example, who, in the words of Robert MacNamara, are living "in situations so deprived as to be below any rational definition of human decency." Or the 17 million children who die each year: many of whom could be saved by the expenditure of relatively small sums on basic health care.

The simple fact is that we are in danger of becoming moral abstainers. Of course Britain's aid flows, public and private, are not inconsiderable, of course they compare rather well even with those of much richer countries and are positively generous compared with the efforts of some countries. But this is to miss the point. The fact is that we simply do not give enough, in absolute or relative terms, to those who need our help. Many noble noises are made, but when the organ stops the collection plate remains rather bare.

This is a bleak note on which to end: but I cannot in all honesty do other-wise: for at least half the population of the planet, the world is a very bleak place. By ignoring the moral dimensions of the problems we risk making it bleaker still, and for ourselves also. I do not believe that members of governments, any more than ordinary citizens, can go on indefin-ately without mental breakdown either individually or collectively unless they have a sense that they are behaving morally. I have tried to address my brief as a religious leader; but I have voiced the anxiety of many that I represent - and I believe that there are several palpable examples in the world today of rational politicians underestimating the strength of religious convictions.

The Prime Minister and the government have shown the capacity to act ener-getically and undaunted by difficulties when convinced that a policy is right and necessary. Let them do so again for the sake of those who face not a loss of their freedom, but the loss of their very lives. In 1947 an American government looked at a Europe devastated by 5 years of war. They decided that for half a decade they would give away 2 per cent of their national income. The Marshall Plan revived Europe, exorcised the spirit of stagnation and defeat, and at the same time fostered expansion and prosper-ity in America as well. Christian concern is a good basis for action. We need nothing less than a new Marshall Plan, and how fine a thing it would be were the energy and commitment for such a plan to come from Britain.

Chapter 10

Reflections on our Response to the Poorest of the Third World

Professor Hans Singer, Emeritus Professor, University of
Sussex; Professorial Fellow, Institute of Development
Studies, Sussex

To cover all the issues raised by the various contributions in considering
our response to the poorest of the Third World would be a much too ambitious
task so I will concentrate on a few points which seem to me most important.
Development education is one issue on which there was a lot of emphasis
and agreement. One approach is to argue that we must get away from rhetoric
and consider concrete action.

But development education is presumably part of rhetoric. It has a
rhetorical element in it, to talk to people, to persuade people, to convince
people, to inspire people, that is part of rhetoric. Therefore the statement that rhetoric is bad and we are past rhetoric and we must now concentrate on concrete action might need further consideration. I might perhaps
also speak as one who has a vested interest in the business of development
education. The role of the universities was not particularly emphasised by
the contributors but I would add to the cut in appropriations for development
education, the increase in the fees for overseas students, which I think has
been a particularly harmful and short-sighted measure. I do hope that when
there is pressure from popular public opinion to look into the issue of
development education again, that the question of the overseas students will
not be neglected.

Clearly, the central piece of the contributions was the question of mutual
interest versus morality. And connected with this, there was, as several
contributors pointed out, the surprising emphasis given to mutual interest
in the Brandt Report. The Brandt Report of course is the main argument for
saying we must be finished with rhetoric, and we must get on to action,
because in the Brandt Report we have already a programme which many people
co-operated in drawing up. A very moderate programme produced by a group in
which people from many countries and many different interests were represented, and which gives us a background from which we could start. The
Brandt Report of course has a special chapter on mutual interest, and that
chapter starts off with the statement "the principle of mutual interest is
of central importance to our Report" but actually as you go on reading
through this chapter, the chapter ends with a final paragraph with a sub-
heading MORALITY. In other words as the chapter goes on it arrives at the
realisation that mutual self-interest takes us only a certain part of the
way. We start by pursuing all areas of discussion where mutual interest

exists, when we ourselves can benefit, and where we can play positive-sum-games. This may be the answer to the deadlocked North-South dialogue. We start with easy problems where our own interest is apparent, which may then help to break the ice, and to get discussion on more important subjects going.

When we talk about North-South dialogue which is also the subtitle of the Brandt Report, we must be aware that there is some contradiction between the idea of a North-South dialogue and concentration on the poorest count-ries because the North-South dialogue presumes an idea of North versus South, and South presupposes that there is a homogeneous South. As observed by Sir Reay Geddes, an important factor is the principle of gradu-ation. As a result of the successful Bretton Woods period and the economic growth which we enjoyed for 25 years or more as a result of this, of what in retrospect looks like golden years, we now have a number of countries which are no longer all that poor, and which could do a lot for their own poor or which indeed could do a lot for the poor of poorer countries. They could join the list of Brandt donors, and therefore we must concentrate on the poorest countries. But when we concentrate on the poorest countries, self-interest does not take us very far because, except perhaps for the provision of important primary commodities, the normal self-interest activity especially in trade, commerce and finance does not really reach the poorest countries. When we come to the poorest countries we must go beyond immediate self-interest.

I emphasise *immediate* self-interest because one of the things I have found very distressing, and which the contributors brought out clearly, is that the term self-interest is not particularly helpful. There is direct commercial self-interest, in the strict business sense. It is one of the paradoxical obstacles with which we struggle, that today, when we have depression and unemployment in our own countries, aid that we give to the poorest countries would be very cheap if the aid helps us to bring our own resources which are now idle into operation, than in fact the aid does not cost us anything, the aid is costless. But on the other hand our self-perception of our own interests leads us to a different proposition. When we ourselves are suffering from troubles we must first put our own house in order, we must help our own people before we can presume to help other people. So there is a paradox which we must somehow make public opinion realise. Although it looks from the surface as if the present times of trouble for ourselves are the worst possible times to think about aid to the poorest countries, yet in actual fact any Keynesian economist would agree that they are the *best* times for thinking about aid to developing countries.

Another important problem for development education is to clearly disting-uish between short term and long term interest. If India attains *per capita* income levels more or less similar to what we have today I am sure this would be a positive-sum-game for everybody in the world - the same for China and obviously the same for the poor of Africa. There is also the question of improving our own perception of our interests to attain such a thing as enlightened self-interest and long-term interest, particularly in a country like the UK, which through history and fate has been put at the centre of so many international affairs and contacts, was a pioneer of the industrial revolution and the welfare state, and through Keynes was the creator of the Bretton Woods System, which gave us 25/30 good years, and helped to solve at least the fringes of the development problem.

There is from the point of view of the Third World, although Mr. Mkona did not use the phrase in his contribution, an opportunity for a New International Economic Order. Many of the things that are needed today that seem very revolutionary and go under the heading of the new international economic order we do not want to discuss because it gives the impression that the old order was all wrong. We do not like the way it is being presented and the whole idea of a homogeneous group of 77 putting forward new policy proposals is harmful to the necessary consideration of the poorest countries. There may be some substance in these concerns, but when you examine their demands for a new international economic order, to somebody who has watched development events for quite some time, they have a surprisingly old-fashioned ring. Some of us actually took part in those moves advocated at Bretton Woods at the end of the last war when there were opportunities to start from scratch, to create a new system because the old system had simply disappeared. We may get to that stage again, but we are not there yet. At that time we were clearly at the point of creating a new international economic system, not tackling problems within the framework of the existing order.

The original ideas that were then put forward for the new international economic order included an International Trade Organisation which was negotiated in Havana in 1946/47. I took part in this as a very young and low-ranking UN staff member. The ITO (International Trade Organisation) was successfully negotiated but unfortunately not ratified by the US Congress so it never was created. However, the ITO could have created stable commodity prices. In fact the world currency would have been based not on gold but on a bundle of commodities. If that had happened the poorest countries of today who depend so largely on export of primary commodities, would not have suffered the catastrophic declines which they have now suffered. The situation would be much more manageable, and there would have been a network of commodity agreements. What in the event happened was the creation of GATT and UNCTAD, and the UNCTAD Common Fund (which Britain resisted so much and which now exists only in embryonic form), and yet all these things are only pale shadows of what was actually proposed at Bretton Woods which we tried to negotiate, but it did not come off.

Another inspiration of Keynes at Bretton Woods, and to some extent also the idea of the American negotiators, was that the burden of economic adjustment should not fall on the countries that are in balance of payments deficit, which today includes all the poorest countries. The burden of adjustment should be on the already-established countries. The proposition then was that it is the surplus countries which by definition create deficits for other countries in the world. It is not possible to have some countries with surpluses without having some other countries with deficits. That is pocket calculator economics although we do not even need a pocket calculator for proving this reality. It is the countries with balance of payments surpluses which should carry the burden of adjustment through expansion, lending, and in other ways. If that principle had been accepted and acted upon, the pressure to adjust would not have been on the developing countries. The pressure would have been on OPEC and Germany, and Japan and other balance of payments surplus countries to take the expansionary and other actions, that would be needed to rectify the situation.

The Bretton Woods proposals also included that of a World Central Bank which would regulate the supply of money not on a monetarist national basis, not on M1, M2 and M3, but on a global basis. Again we have an embryonic application of this idea, in that Special Drawing Rights, from time to time, are issued by the IMF, but this is only a parody of the ideas put forward at Bretton Woods like GATT being a parody of the ITO. Finally, although this

was not part of Bretton Woods, let me recall the Archbishop of Canterbury's
reference to the Marshall Plan. That was not a part of Bretton Woods but
it was an example of a very enlightened and generous action - the US giving
away something like 3 per cent of its GNP, for 4 years running, and on a
grant basis, not on a loan basis. We could argue that it would have been
better for the world if the Americans had not been quite so generous. If
the Marshall Plan had been on a loan basis, and if the Marshall Plan had to
be repaid with ample interest at current interest rates, and repayments
could be recycled today to the poorest countries, the problem of the poorest
countries would be a long way towards a solution. From this view point the
problem is due to our failure to respond to the US action of the Marshall
Plan, by a similar action now in response to the developing countries - yet
another illustration of how our standards of international behaviour seem to
have slipped from the days of 30 years ago. Thus we do not necessarily have
to think in highly revolutionary terms, or about things that we never
thought about or tried to do. If we only went back in many ways to the outlook and action that we tried to pursue at Bretton Woods, at the end of the
last war, many things would look a lot better.

Beyond direct commercial interest, and long term enlightened interest, we
have the problem of what the Brandt Report calls "the common heritage of
mankind." There are many things that are the common heritage of mankind -
the environment is one thing, outer space, the ocean floor. We have a joint
common task as human species that we could so much more effectively pursue
together. Disarmament could also be part of the common goal of peace; peace
is certainly part of our common heritage, if we can achieve it. One common
heritage which was only referred to indirectly by the contributors is the
human infrastructure as distinct from commercial capital which goes into
directly productive projects in the poorest countries. The problem of
human infrastructure includes one of the great problems of a common heritage,
namely the common action needed, whether you call it self-interest or
morality is an open question, towards children. Surely that too is human
infrastructure, both for the countries into which these children are born,
but also for us as a human species together.

Children are our future and 90 per cent of all children are born in developing countries. In the poorest countries of course the birth rate is even
higher than in other developing countries, and the average child is much
poorer than the average adult because large families are one of the main
causes of poverty. The lower down you go on the income cycle from urban to
rural areas the higher the birth rate. The great majority of children, who
are our common heritage, on which our hopes rest, are affected by malnutrition and vicious circular interaction between malnutrition, poor health and
poverty. They are affected by this interaction to such a degree that their
mental and physical development is in great danger. Unfortunately malnutrition of children is not infectious, so we do not have any reason to help in
the eradication of malnutrition, as we have a direct self-interest in the
eradication of cholera, because cholera may come back and affect us. Even
if the diseases, and illnesses that are introduced, are interrelated with
malnutrition, they will not always come back to us. Action on behalf of the
world's children is automatically concentrated on the poorest, because the
children are the poorest. It does represent long term and enlightened self-
interest because we all will depend on our future Newtons and Einsteins and
other geniuses and technicians to help us to cope with the problems of the
next century and beyond. But 90 per cent of these potential Newtons and
Einsteins are being born in developing countries, in circumstances where
they will die before they can become Newtons and Einsteins, or they may be
illiterate, or they get so little food below the age of 3 that their brain

does not fully develop.

Investment in the world's children is one of the areas which if I put all
the strands of thought of the foregoing contributions together seems to me
to be an area which combines everything. It also has the great advantage
of appealing to public opinion as a very popular subject. Children are
presumably non-controversial subjects, and therefore public opinion should
also be more easily roused, in this particular type of development education
than others. But there remains the problem that however far you stretch the
principle of mutual interest to include action for children because we need
the potential Newtons and Einsteins, since 90 per cent are not born in our
own countries but in developing countries, there comes a point where self-
interest stops. We all must recognise this, because at the other extreme of
that scale of self-interest and morality, none of us hesitate when there is
a real emergency. If there is an earthquake or a typhoon or a terrible
famine, then the international agencies do operate, and gifts do pour in,
action is being taken, although often limited by transport difficulties or
by ignorance. It seems to me that the missing link between self-interest
stretched as far as it will go at one end, and emergencies when we do not
talk much of self-interest but try to help if possible, was the idea which
His Grace the Archbishop of Canterbury and other contributors mentioned,
that prevention is always much better, cheaper, and more helpful to everybody concerned, than cure. Early action to prevent famines, and to prevent
emergencies from being beyond the capacity of whole communities to deal
with, and leading to wholesale deaths, might be one of these connecting
links.

Index

62